CORFU S

Avrio never comes

John Waller

Illustrations by
John Chipperfield

YIANNIS BOOKS
England

YIANNIS BOOKS

Acknowledgements

I thank my friends and family who have supported me in this project and to David for his editing. I thank the many readers of Greek Walls who have asked "when do we get the sequel?"

Published in 2005 by **YIANNIS BOOKS**
Strawberry Vale, Twickenham TW1 4SJ, UK

Typeset by Mike Cooper, 25 Orchard Rd, Sutton SM1 2QA, UK
Printed by Antony Rowe, Chippenham, Wiltshire, UK

232pp
ISBN 0-9547887-1-0

Corfu Sunset

Avrio never comes

Plan of project

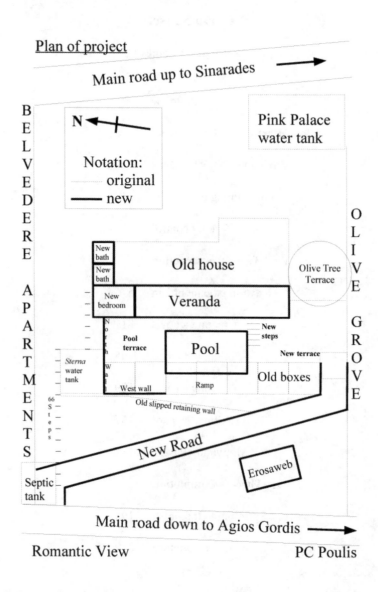

Main road up to Sinarades →

N ←

Notation:
...... original
—— new

Pink Palace
water tank

BELVEDERE APARTMENTS

OLIVE GROVE

New
bath

New
bath

New
bedroom

Old house

Olive Tree
Terrace

Veranda

North Wall

Pool
terrace

New
steps

Pool

New terrace

Sterna
water
tank

West wall

Ramp

Old boxes

66 Steps

Old slipped retaining wall

New Road

Septic
tank

Erosaweb

Main road down to Agios Gordis →

Romantic View

PC Poulis

For Nikos 'Mechanikos' Papavlassopoulos
And the great Greek workers

THE CHARACTERS

THE LOCALS

Spiros 'Belvedere Apartments' Grammenos	Our neighbour
Dr. George 'Pink Palace' Grammenos	Son of:
Spiros 'Pink Palace' Grammenos	Pink Palace founder
George 'Texaco' (now Shell) Grammenos	Source of all information
Caroline	George Texaco's wife
George 'Georgy Porgy' Grammenos	Sinarades taverna owner
Fotis and Tassos Doukakis	Of Theodoros taverna
Michael and	Of Romantic View and
Anna Pangalis	Romantic Palace
Spiros 'Mini-market' Mazis	Elected local councillor
Councillor Nikos Papadatos	Councillor
PC Poulis	Neighbour below
Spiros and son Alekos Alamanos	Community plumbers

THE WORKERS

Petros Kardakis	Original engineer
Spiros Zervos	Petros Kardakis's partner
Nikos 'Mechanikos' Papavlassopoulos	Our engineer
and Anna	and his architect wife
Zacharias	Our first wall builder
Nikos 'Bulldozer' Grammenos	Hero Hellenic Republic
Pavlos (Paul Newman)	Final wall builder
George (Segal)	Pavlos's partner
Nikos 'Builder' Merianos	The best builder in the area
Marinos	Lorry driver and waiter
Alexos Hirdaris	Rep. of pool company
Polish Valdek, Christos, Albanian Christos	Swimming pool installers
Vassilis Proskyr/Yiannis	Concrete provider/manager
Spiros Moskou and Sasha	Tile provider and secretary

THE OTHERS

Agalis and Rob	Daughter and son-in-law of:
Elena Manessis	Friend for 35 years
Costas Tsivanides	Our lawyer
Amalia	Our accountant
Fred	Lumberjack and gardener

Looking back from below the mountain of Garouna to our once virgin hillside, we were shocked, appalled and dazed by a great Pink City that had grown up behind the Pink Palace. Spiros 'Pink Palace' Grammenos had come a long way in twenty-five years. It was impossible to be too angry with the development as it had provided a 'home away from home' for tens of thousands of students, many from the United States. I was sure that they would always have happy memories of our lovely island.

PROLOGUE

Wednesday 13 June 2001

Seven beeps and a long blast on the horn: are we sinking? I'm not usually superstitious, but it is the 13th of the month. My mind leaps back to last year, when a Minoan High Speed Ferry hit an island in the Aegean and sank. I haven't felt anything and I don't think there are any islands here in the middle of the Adriatic, but I'm still worried. My wife and I follow the green 'family group' signs, and arrive on deck. Phew! We can relax again. Minoan Lines is just having a lifeboat drill. The crew, who are wearing life jackets, wander around, looking bored. It seems that they should be looking for passengers in their cabins but, today, they miss this job out. Instead, they meet up with those who want to see the display and have a discussion. Greeks are good at having discussions.

Someone points to a lifeboat but the officer replies: "No, we won't launch one today".

This is not because they don't know how to - I'm sure they do. Nor because it would spoil the paint - it's because we have to beat the rival Strintzis Lines. Why on earth both lines are scheduled to leave Venice at the same time and arrive in Greece at the same time has always baffled me.

This time we win the race. Jannie and I take this as a good omen, as we too are engaged in a race. At the same time as the Greek government is struggling to complete its mammoth Olympic construction project in three years time, we are starting on our own Olympian project in Corfu - three months to build a road up the mountain to our villa and re-roof it, construct a swimming pool and build a veranda and an extension.

We will then have a home to match the beauty of the island and our idyllic situation, surrounded by olive tree covered mountains above the long sandy beach of Agios Gordis, overlooking the open Mediterranean to the west.

I think back two years to when we decided to renovate our house.

PART ONE - PREPARATION

Making new Greek friends

A week after my retirement in April 1999, Jannie and I flew to Athens on Easyjet, hired a car and drove up to Corfu. With more time on our hands, we wanted to see whether we could live in our house outside the main tourist season.

For years we had visited the island for just a couple of weeks each summer. When we built the little villa thirty years ago, we called it '*Iliovasilema*', 'Sunset'. Then a neighbour, Spiros Grammenos, arrived to the north. He built his guest house 'Belvedere Apartments' jutting out from the mountain, rising four storeys from the road below and blocking out the sunset in July and August. As we looked towards the dying sun, we would see Spiros, spying at us from the bridge of his ugly construction.

Arriving at the house late at night, we had our usual concerns. Any Albanians squatters in residence? No. Any electricity? Yes. I should have been relieved but I feared this was going too well.

We went into the sitting room and looked aghast at a long trail of dust, one centimetre high. We had been invaded. The trail led us to the spare room, the one that was eaten by termites many years before. We saw a large brown lump on the bed. Then it dawned on us, the lump was part of the roof. Something had been up under the tiles, eating the timbers. We entered our bedroom. No tell-tale trails or lumps, but a column of ants entering and leaving the light switch above the bed. Jannie switched the light on – and we heard the hiss of thousands of ants being electrocuted. However, the intruders had the last laugh. The light went out; the ants had shorted the switch.

As I fell asleep I decided that, for us to live in Corfu in the spring and autumn, we must first of all replace our sieve with a new roof. But this would cost money, which was more of a problem now that I was not working. Living on a pension demanded economies and Stelios's excellent Easyjet airline was the first. Our second saving was a visit to Fast Food Vassilis in Pelekas, the village to the north of our own, Sinarades. The red gingham clothed bistro tables, delightful décor – garlands of plastic vines over a multitude of mini-mirrors – and soothing Greek music welcomed us. But it was the two course meal *for two* that completely won us over. Including half a litre of wine, it cost *only £2.80*. We could live here for ever.

Vassilis was charming, Eleni was delightful – as a regular I had earned a peck on both cheeks – and their twin girls were perfect. One looked like her father; the other like her mother. Not surprisingly perhaps, they didn't appear in the 1999 Egon Ronay Food Guide. The starter – pita bread and tzatziki – and the main course – chicken, sausage or pork with chips, salad and home-made tomato sauce – were combined in a convenient package. But who cared at that price. The house wine tasted like a Chardonnay, but it couldn't have been as Vassilis had grown the grapes. The music was classical – clarinets from the mountains of Epirus.

Greece, we were now to discover, is different before the tourists arrive. April is the walking and talking time of year. We walked to Pentati, the village we can see across the bay from the villa. Spring flowers lined the lane; butterflies – their wings still pristine – flitted from bloom to bloom; cicadas started to rustle; lizards lazed in the sun. Everything was bliss – almost.

Looking back from below the mountain of Garouna to our once virgin hillside, we were shocked, appalled and dazed by a great Pink City that had grown up behind the Pink Palace.

This was hidden at road level by the two storey replacement to the original roadside building, which sat on an enormous retaining wall, perhaps eight metres high at the downhill end. For the first time, up high, we could now see its offspring, pink blocks containing hundreds of rooms for backpackers. From afar the complex appeared to have eight storeys. At least all the blocks had pitched roofs tiled in the traditional fashion. Spiros 'Pink Palace' Grammenos had come a long way in twenty-five years. It was impossible to be too angry with the development as it had provided a 'home away from home' for tens of thousands of students, many from the United States. I was sure that they would always have happy memories of our lovely island.

We filled up with petrol at the Texaco service station on the ridge between Sinarades and Agios Gordis. As it was April, the owner had time to talk. He introduced himself as George Grammenos. His name didn't surprise us as half the villagers of Sinarades had the same surname. George was short, swarthy and unshaven with a roguish twinkle in his eyes. I congratulated him on his excellent English.

"I married an English girl," he explained. He smiled at a tall, willowy and pretty young brunette, with a broad smile, who had just walked in. "This is Caroline, my wife."

"We met when I was working at the Pink Palace," she added.

"I am John and this is Jannie, we've had a house here for twenty-seven years."

"Never!" he said.

I explained that we had spent only a week or two each year since the early seventies.

"Who do you know then?" he asked.

"Scarcely anyone in the village, but we are good friends of the Manessis family."

Of the three brothers, it was the youngest, George, who had taken us under his wing when we arrived in 1966. He managed the Avis rental side of the family business, while the middle brother Theodore ran the Mobil garage and Fiat concessionaires. The eldest, Stephen, who maintained the family estate at Benitses, was the only one still alive.

"I used to work at the Mobil service station when I was young," said George. Corfu is a small world.

"We are also friends of Petros Kardakis." Petros had built our house and he had also visited us in England.

"He's a good engineer," commented George.

I stopped.

"And anyone else?" he asked.

"We know Spiros Grammenos, of Belvedere Apartments, who is our next door neighbour. But we have some problems with him."

"So!" he said with a laugh. Perhaps we weren't the only ones who did, but he wasn't letting on.

"And Spiros Grammenos of the Pink Palace, who is just down the road from us."

"He's my cousin. Anyone else?"

"No."

"Well it's about time you did," he said.

"Start with another of George's cousins," suggested Caroline. "He's just opened a kebab place in the village. It is very clean and the food is good."

"And walk with the villagers to Kouramades on Sunday," suggested George.

We did. We followed the saint of the village, whose remains were being carried in a cask. The procession was led by the priests, holding aloft great crosses – some with paintings of religious scenes attached. It seemed the whole of Sinarades walked behind – very slowly, to the sombre music of the village band. We trailed at the back – intruders at this solemn and personal affair.

The brass instruments and musicians' helmets glinted in the morning sun. The vineyards were a mass of pale pink cranesbill. Along our route, Judas trees were in blossom – a deeper shade of pink. For a thousand years, Greeks had celebrated their saints' days in the same way. All the men were in suits and many of the women wore black.

Walking at a snail's pace gave us more time to look around. Above the column and beyond the valley rose Agii Deka, the highest mountain in the centre of the island. On its summit sat what looked like a great white golf ball. It wasn't there last year. The owner of the little supermarket down the road, Spiros Mazis, came up and welcomed us.

"I'm glad you could come. Today is important for the villagers."

He walked up the line, saying hello and shaking hands. I wondered if he was canvassing. I used to do the same when I was in British politics in the 1970s and 1980s.

We turned off the main road and wound our way up to the neighbouring village of Kouramades. The crawl slowed and then stopped. The heart of the village was so narrow that a car couldn't have passed through. After well over an hour we returned to the outskirts of Sinarades and the procession went up to the cemetery for a service. We thought we had done our duty and quietly left.

The following day, we took Caroline's advice and went for a kebab in the village. We sat down at one of the three minute tables inside. The owner came over. He was a handsome bronzed man in his late forties.

"Caroline said we should come," I started, hoping we would get special treatment. I needn't have worried.

"I'm Georgy Porgy," he said. His smile was captivating. His eyes were full of life.

I laughed. "Now, what is your real name?"

"Georgy Porgy. The English all called me that when I worked at the Yaliskari Hotel."

It was a joke that would amuse most people – once. I could see how the tourists – particularly the women – would have been enchanted. The Greek male has a native attraction to the British; they are open and full of fun.

"But what is your *real* name?" I insisted.

"OK, it's George."

"And your other name?"

"Grammenos."

I should have guessed. We already knew two Spiros Grammenoses. Now we had met two George Grammenoses. Having expected just kebabs, we were in for a surprise. The giro was rotating, the meat was sizzling on the grill and chicken was browning on the spit. In case that wasn't enough, he offered us *bifteki* – his wife's homemade hamburgers.

"Chicken," said Jannie.

"Make it two," I added.

They were succulent and served with tzatziki, salad and crisp fresh chips. After one bite, Jannie said. "I'm adding this to our taverna list."

Georgy Porgy had bought us a half litre of wine – it was interesting. He came over to ask us how we liked the wine.

"Excellent," we replied in unison.

"I make it myself," he said. "I mix Kakotrygis, a white wine, with Petrokorintho, a red one."

I didn't tell him I had been warned about mixing drinks. At the next table was a slightly inebriated local with a litre of George's wine – confirming that the warning was justified.

"I'm Spiros," he introduced himself in a Brooklyn accent. "They call me Amerikanos. I came back to Corfu last year and I work as a cook at Yaliskari in the summer. I saw you in the parade on Sunday."

George 'Texaco' Grammenos was right – if we wanted to meet the villagers, walk to Kouramades.

"How do you like the restaurant?" he asked, using a word which was slightly over the top.

"It's great." I replied, trying not to grin stupidly.

"I planned everything for George," he added.

So this was how he got his litre of wine – as a daily consultancy fee.

"George's wine *ish* not *ash* good *ash* mine," he confided in me, slightly slurring his words. "Mine's the real stuff," he added. He sounded like the owner of a speak-easy in prohibition America. "I make a thousand litres a year, I'll get you some."

At this point, with great care, he got up and staggered off up the street. A few minutes later, he returned with a five litre bottle, filled with a murky liquid.

"Tell me what you think of it, next time you come here."

So this was how one made friends in Sinarades.

Back home, I surveyed the jungle beside the road. It was now over head height and impenetrable. Next to the steps climbing up to the house was what I called my 'lawn' – a small patch of tall luscious green grass in need of a trim. While I was cutting it with a pair of scissors and saying "hello" to passers-by as part of my 'getting to know the locals' venture, a man came up and introduced himself.

"I'm Nikos Papadatos and I live down the road. I saw you in Kouramades – thank you for coming."

He was in his early fifties and unsmiling. I sensed a man of authority – I found out later that he was a local councillor.

"You have a problem!" he said in an unfriendly and officious way. He pointed first at my 'drive in' where our car was parked and then at the pipe under the ramp up to it.

"There."

I looked and saw a large turd, right next to my lawn. Maybe our neighbour, Spiros Grammenos, had got another Alsatian. Fifteen years before, his dogs had driven off the estate agent when we tried to sell the property. I wasn't an expert on faeces, I must confess.

"Spiros says it's your shit."

I laughed. "I come here for two weeks a year, and you say it's mine. That's rubbish. If it's anyone's it's Spiros's."

It was his turn to be confused. He departed perplexed.

Another man came up. I'd seen him in the Romantic View – across the road from us where he had some rooms to let.

"I'm your neighbour, Michael Pangalis. Don't believe Papadatos – he's one of those politicians. The problem is Spiros Grammenos. He lets his septic tank overflow all through the winter."

"Where's his septic tank, then?" I asked.

"Under your car!"

"But that's my land," I said.

"Then you should blow up his tank," he said, meaning every word.

I looked up at Spiros's and saw a face peeping out from behind his latest upward extension which gave him a bird's eye view of my property and Michael's below. Michael left as some workmen had just arrived to work on his new building.

Moments later, Spiros rushed down his stairs.

"Good morning, Mr. Wallace."

"Why is your septic tank on my land?" I asked him.

He pretended not to answer, so I pointed at the turd.

"That's yours," I said angrily.

"No, Mr. Wallace. All mine is on the other side of the house."

He took me up the road and showed me the drain pipes. One of the advantages of Greek construction was that all services, in and out, were in full view. I was now even more confused.

"Michael says there is a tank under my car," I suggested.

"No, Mr. Wallace. Michael is a very bad man. He wants to build a hotel there with five storeys. I say Mr. Wallace, the Englishman, won't see the sea. So now it will have only three storeys. You are pleased with me, yes?"

Maybe George Texaco had been wrong. I didn't want to know anyone else. Sinarades was a battleground. Perhaps we should mix with old friends such as Elena Manessis and Petros Kardakis. Elena, the widow of George who nurtured our love for the island and kept our spirits up throughout our long fight with our neighbour, was a dear friend. Like many well educated Greeks of her generation, who had lived through the tragedy of German occupation in the war and the Civil War that followed, she was trim and strong. Her still beautiful face was lined perhaps by the memories of her youth and her thick hair was turning grey, but she still had the bounce of one much younger. She always had a twinkle in her eyes and a soft and welcoming smile.

Petros, on the other hand, was now showing his age. Tall, elegant and proud, he was one of the top engineers on the island. He had built our house and together we had shared the pleasure of its creation. He invited us out to the yacht club. He told us about his sailing, to which he was addicted. We asked him about the weird golf ball we had seen on top of Agii Deka on our walk to Kouramades. He told us that it was radar to help aircraft land blind at Corfu Airport.

"You know how hard it is sometimes for pilots coming from the south – the runway appears between a mountain on one side and a hill on the other," he said with the authority of one living under the flight path at Perama. "The 'golf ball' is to help pilots land, just on instruments. Well, the villagers at Agii Deka didn't like it," he continued. "One night they climbed up the mountain and vandalised the radar equipment – they were afraid of the radiation."

Jannie was going pale at this explanation. "The villagers are crazy! Many years ago, we were approaching the runway at night in a storm. Lightning was flashing; everyone was scared," she said. "At the last moment, the pilot aborted the landing and we had to return to Athens. I am for anything that will help the pilots." She turned to me. "You know, John, how flying has always scared me. Petros has confirmed why I want us to drive to Greece now we have the time."

"Does that mean we will see more of you?" asked Petros, excitedly.

"We plan to spend spring and autumn here," she said. "It's too hot in the summer. But first we must fix up the house and get mains water."

"Water won't be a problem. I'll apply for you tomorrow," he offered. He then told us about Profi, the technical supermarket, the favourite haunt of DIYers – which until then we hadn't visited. He said it sold everything we needed to fix the house.

"Come over one afternoon with Miranda when we get the water and we will celebrate," I suggested. That also appealed to him.

We later took Elena out to Poulades to check on progress at her daughter Agalis's house. It had been plastered and painted. She was thrilled with our news. Though she had many friends, she was pleased there was someone else with whom she could go to remote beaches. As she didn't drive, she had been missing her regular expeditions with George.

"What's the first project?" she asked with a laugh. She knew I had to have targets all the time.

"We need mattresses," Jannie replied. "The four in the bunk room have disintegrated and the one in the spare room is mouldy."

She told us of a shop at the bottom of the steps to the Cathedral. It was closed when we went, but a helpful neighbour gave us directions to the *ergostasio* north of Corfu Town. I checked in my pocket dictionary and found the translation was 'factory'. The island was famous for olive oil and tourism, but it seemed extraordinary that it also manufactured mattresses. But sure enough, beside the main road, we found *Imperial Strom* in a large concrete building.

We were welcomed by the receptionist. She was a Greek speaker from Agii Saranda in Albania, whose education system couldn't have been too bad, as her English too was excellent. We ordered full length sprung mattresses, four 65cm wide and one 130cm wide. These weird measurements didn't worry her as everything was made to measure. We were offered two grades – standard and special – with an optional extra of a guarantee against insect infiltration. At the prices she quoted, we went for the whole works: country living in Corfu meant cohabiting with creepy crawlies. We picked them up a week later, tied them to the top of the minute rental car and crept across the island.

"Twenty-first century, here we come," Jannie announced.

On our last full day, the mains arrived in the morning and Petros and Miranda came in the afternoon. It is remarkable how quickly things can happen in Greece, if you know the right people. The only disappointment was that we wouldn't be able to drink the water as it came from Sinarades and was of doubtful purity. Across the valley to the south, water from the mountain of Garouna was excellent to drink.

Our meal, normally carefree, was subdued. Petros's business life was collapsing. He had invested his own money in a shopping mall at Alepou. It had been a disaster and his debts had built up. Even his boat would have to go to pay off his creditors.

On the international front, he was devastated.

"Three and half years ago, Clinton used Milosovic to bring the war in Bosnia to an end. He was then the hero. Now you are bombing Serbia into the dark ages. I accept that Milosevic mistreated the Kosovan Albanians, but you didn't say anything then. Now you are killing thousands of Serbs – you are just as bad as him."

For a Greek, Serbia was more than just another Orthodox country. They had been friends since the First World War, when the Serbian Army, an ally of Britain, had marched over the Albanian mountains to Corfu. For Petros, what made things worse was NATO's bombing of Montenegro, a neutral in the Balkan conflict, where his mother's family came from.

We climbed the steps from the beach and entered Theodoros's, unchanged in all those years. In my excellent 'food ordering' Greek, I asked for two beers.

"You speak our language," replied the owner, a dark haired, athletic looking man in his mid thirties. "Where are you staying?"

"We've had a house on the road to Sinarades for nearly thirty years."

I had touched a raw nerve.

20

Entertaining old friends

The forty years I had spent in the computer business had taught me that success came from spending as much time as possible on defining the requirements of a system. This was my excuse for not rushing in to the renovation of Iliovasilema; rather than the truth – no money. Nevertheless it was time to find out what our friends and family would want. If they liked the end product, they would be more inclined to come to Corfu. We chose two couples, each with different ideas of a perfect holiday. We would balance their views with those of our children. Could the island and our house satisfy them all?

The economies of flying and hiring a car became unattractive as soon as we decided to stay for two months so we decided to drive. Czuk, a flatmate from bachelor days, and his wife Lucy joined us on the outward journey in September 1999. We compared the longer drive to Brindisi, which we had made in 1966, and its shorter, therefore cheaper, ferry across to Corfu against the two day drive to Venice and the twenty-four hour ferry. It was no contest. Venice, the most romantic of cities, had to win.

Venice, as always, was captivating, especially when viewed from high above the houses from the deck of a huge ferry which was guided by a tug boat down Giudecca's Canal past the entrance to the Grand Canal and St. Mark's Square. By the time we had arrived at the Lido and the open Adriatic, I had chosen the building where we would rent a room – such was the fantasy of the moment.

Back in Corfu, we returned from our first shopping trip with vast quantities of water, wine and beer. We were faced with the sixty-six steps up to the house. Czuk, a short, round and always happy Pole with white hair, whose mountaineering ability depended solely on the food and wine at the other end, carried himself up with some choice delicacies which he had found in town. Lucy, dark, vivacious and of recent Irish descent, was chatting with Jannie. They followed with a plastic bag in each hand. The Sherpa trailed behind with the litres of drink. At that moment, I decided that our first requirement had to be a road up to the house for the less able and for me, the beast of burden. My effort was rewarded as Czuk served us a non-stop selection of salads and starters. Given a kitchen larger than a yacht's galley, Lucy would also have been cooking some delicacies.

We soon realised that these friends wanted more than the beautiful countryside and beaches of the island. They loved culture and, particularly, museums. An early trip took us to the monastery at Paleokastritsa. Our guests were captivated by the peace of the little chapel and the majesty of its location above the deep blue Mediterranean. Greeks are a strongly religious people and they respect their Orthodox traditions. Our next monastery was on the top of Mount Pantokrator, the highest point on the island, from where one could see the sun set to the west and the moon rise in the east. With monks no longer in residence, it was now operated by a smart local and a horde of Albanians who insisted that, for the sake of respect, long skirts be put on by those tourists, male and female, that wore shorts – for a fee. A few years before, on our visit to Meteora, the unbelievable mainland monasteries perched on high rocks above the Thessalian plain, the monks had been offended when a friend had wanted to tip them for his skirt. Times were changing. Yet there was even hope here as we noted the start of a renovation project. Scaffolding had been erected and the ceiling was being cleaned to reveal beautiful paintings.

Our next destination was the Achillion Palace, constructed in 1890 for Empress Elizabeth of Austria. Sissy, as she was called by her family, was one of Corfu's early tourists. Twenty years before, on her first visit, she fell in love with the island and its people. She chose her site well – on a hilltop near Gastouri – with views of Mouse Island and the town to the north. Until she was assassinated in 1898, she spent her springs and late summers at the Palace. In 1907, Kaiser Wilhelm II bought the property and altered it to his Imperial tastes, a project which included the erection of a five metre high bronze sculpture of the 'Victorious Achilles'.

We queued for our tickets – there were a dozen tour buses unloading their passengers. We climbed the steps to the great pseudo-classical edifice and entered under enormous columns. The hall was crowded – a hundred squawking visitors gaped up, mouths open like chicks waiting to be fed, at the fresco on the ceiling depicting a pastoral scene with naked nymphs cavorting. Ahead was the great marble staircase, at the top of which the imperial hosts would once have stood.

Czuk was in his element. With his knowledge of German, he could have spent a whole day just reading the memorabilia of the Empress and the Kaiser. Outside, there was a colonnade with statues of the great philosophers and writers of all time, including Shakespeare.

On their last day, we again sat out under the great olive tree on our terrace and discussed their requirements. Through the poplar trees which we had planted thirty years before, they caught mere glimpses of the dazzling sea, reflecting the sun above. We all voted the trees should go. To compensate for the loss of trees in front, we would plant twenty cypresses behind the house.

"We'd also like somewhere to cook you hot meze," suggested Czuk. The Calor gas cooker had long since rusted away. "You have German and Italian supermarkets as well as Greek. The food we can buy is fantastic and the fruit and vegetables are so fresh."

"And can we go to Mon Repos?" asked Lucy. "I'm sure the memorabilia of its residents, the British colonials then Greek royalty, will not be in German," she added tongue-in-cheek.

(Mon Repos, with its lovely gardens and exquisitely proportioned neo-classical Regency building, is just south of Corfu Town. And what will Lucy find about its main residents? "In 1864, King George 1 named the house 'Mon Repos'. Until 1967 it was the summer house of the Royal Family of Greece." A century of history has been airbrushed out by a republic that has never forgiven King Constantine for his involvement with the *junta*, the dictatorship of the Colonels. The schism between the monarchy and the politicians, which started in 1915, still remains deep in the Greek heart. As a sop to the British tourist, a plaque has been put up at the entrance to 'Prince Philip – born here in 1921'.)

With our friends gone, we wandered the streets of Corfu Town which, with most of the tourists departed, hosted choirs and dancers performing in little Venetian squares. As we walked through the maze of alleys in the Old Town and promenaded along the Liston which had been built by the French at the beginning of the 19th century in the image of the Rue de Rivoli, we decided that, in our older age, this was the Corfu we loved as much as the sea and the countryside.

As crystal clear days and cold starlit nights came in October, cyclamen daubed the glades in the olive trees pink while the occasional yellow sternbergia, of the daffodil family, dazzled the rocky outcrops.

There was great excitement, as elections were coming up in November. Greeks love their politics, the louder the better. Having watched his performance at the Easter parade, we were not surprised that Spiros Mazis, our mini-market man, was standing for the village council. Local government re-organisation on the island had changed the logical regions, North, South, Town and Central, to eleven districts. The bay of Agios Gordis now belonged to three districts, a recipe for indecision and conflict, such as the policy of one, Achilleon, which Spiros claimed took lorry-loads of sand from our beach across the island to the shingle strip in front of Benitses. Spiros was on Councillor Papadatos's list, to the right of and in opposition to that of the PASOK mayor, Vlachos, who was a friend of Petros Kardakis.

I liked Spiros, as I had never heard him shout. With a couple of daughters, he also seemed a very genuine family man. Nikos Papadatos had rebuked me over the 'shit' incident, but I decided that he was just doing what a councillor had to do. I therefore offered Spiros Mazis, the novice, my seventeen years' campaigning skills.

"In England, we would produce a leaflet dealing with local issues and deliver it to all the houses in the voting area," I proposed.

"What sort of issues?" he asked.

"It could mention the loss of our sand and the problems of traffic and parking in the village. We could call it 'Focus on Sinarades'."

"But I wouldn't know how to produce it," he countered.

"I could draw up the artwork and layout and you could write the words," I suggested.

He was mildly interested but questioned the logistical problem of delivering it to every house in the area.

"Leave that to me. Some good friends are due to arrive in a couple of weeks. With their help, Jannie and I could deliver the leaflet."

Perhaps wisely Spiros rejected my proposal. It seemed that, in Greece, it was who you knew that was a gauge of what you could achieve, rather than what you knew. Councillor Papadatos had been the local organiser for the rightist candidate for the Greek Presidency, Konstantinos Stephanopoulos. I accepted that with friends like that, Spiros didn't really need my help. I also think the idea of a tear-off slip for problems and grumbles didn't appeal. He knew he would be visited by many of the villagers, asking for help in exchange for the votes they said they had cast for him.

Our next guests, Henley and Penny, friends since we were first married, had been to Corfu before. He was the perfect companion, easy going with an endless stream of hilarious jokes, which I could never remember. He had just one requirement – really good wine. She, however, keen on an active holiday, wanted to see more of the island and had already planned our week. First on her agenda, we went to Liapades to meet her 'Amerikanos', yet another Brooklyn returnee who, on their previous visit, had chatted her up in the cafenion in the village square when the men were swimming. To her disappointment and our amusement, none of the villagers could remember him.

She then told us of the trip on the caique with a gorgeous Greek captain. They had stopped at a picturesque cove, where she had had a delicious swim and a fantastic meal. As she had forgotten where it was, she agreed to our standard first excursion – Mitsos at Nissaki followed by coffee at Kouloura. We drove around the Corniche. Penny was getting more and more excited.

"The mountain was definitely the one up to the left. I remember that building," she said pointing to the old Red House at Barbati. "I'm sure I saw that beach as well." We turned down the little road to Nissaki and she exclaimed: "John, I know it was here. We definitely came here."

The swim was as good as before; the food was excellent; we found a bottle of wine for Henley; there was even a caique in the cove. Sadly the captain wasn't Penny's. The owner, Agatha, confirmed he did exist – but he hadn't been back for a couple of months. I told her, that if she saw him again, she should tell him that Penny missed him. That was after the second bottle of wine.

To recover from our unsuccessful searches into Penny's interesting past, she and I decided to spend a day on Agios Gordis. The two of us swam for the best part of an hour.

October was the best month for keen swimmers. The water would still be warm and would stay calm for a couple of weeks before a storm crossed the island. It was then exciting to body surf in over the sandbanks.

Henley, as good natured as ever, had watched us for a while and had then wandered off to the south end of the beach. He returned when we came ashore.

"Have I a place for you, John!"

He then extolled the quality of the beer, the beauty of the waitress and the sublime location. While Jannie and Penny read, we crept off for some refreshment. Just before we arrived at 'Henley's Place', I apologised. "Would you mind if we went into this place first – we used to go here when we were young."

In 1966, Theodore Manessis, George's brother, had introduced us to his friend Theodoros Doukakis, who had spent his national service in Theodore's regiment. On his return to Corfu, after time earning some money in Germany, he had set up this little taverna with his wife Olga. We climbed the steps from the beach and entered Theodoros's, unchanged in all those years. In my excellent 'food ordering' Greek, I asked for two beers.

"You speak our language," replied the owner, a dark haired, athletic looking man in his mid thirties. "Where are you staying?"

"We've had a house on the road to Sinarades for nearly thirty years."

I had touched a raw nerve.

"So you are the Englishman," he said threateningly. "When I was a little boy, you came here regularly. Then you didn't. Why not?"

He was very angry.

"Because the beach was crowded," I replied in all honesty.

"Everyday I come past your house from the village – you are never there. I ask myself, what sort of man is this?"

27

"I was busy working in England," I said feebly. "We came most summers."

"So why didn't you come here? When I did my national service in the Army, we were stationed on an island. We always went to the same cafenion. Whenever I go back, I always visit it. It is like that in Athens as well. For fifteen years, I return to the same place."

While he harangued me, Henley's attention was taken by the stunning cook. She was a few years older than our host with blond hair and blue-green eyes. Her fierce nose suggested that she wasn't some northern belle.

"John," said Henley, "I am thirsty."

"So you are John; I am Fotis, Theodoros's son." Pointing to the cook, he added. "And she is Maria, my sister. I'll get the beers."

He returned and carried on his monologue. We drank up quickly and, as we were leaving, I promised him we would be back. It was then that I remembered vaguely the little boy, holding on to his mother's apron, and his older sister who brought us our gazozas when we first visited the beach. I realised that this was a promise I would have to keep.

Each evening, Henley inspected our 'taverna list'. He fell for the 'big kisser' Elisabetha in Doukades, but the evening was a disaster. She was grumpy – it was the end of the season and at 70 she was allowed to be. He said her purple wine was undrinkable – it was now a year old. Penny inspected the kitchen and claimed that it would fail EEC hygiene tests. She then refused to eat her chicken from the pot – it tasted of cinnamon like my lamb. So I drank the litre of wine and ate everyone's food – in Greece it is just not done to offend one's host.

However, Henley adored the 'Five Sisters' Taverna in Mandouki even though there were only four of them there on the night we went. The shelves on the wall were stacked with bottles of Boutari Naoussa, which he approved of. The sisters were as lovely as ever. The meat on the grill was perfect. In return for our hospitality, they then took us to Rex, the classy restaurant on the Liston. The food was good but the price was high.

Before they left, we made an expedition to the northwest of the island. We stopped off first at the Bellavista, above Paleokastritsa. Can there be a more spectacular view around the whole Mediterranean? The ancient graffiti painted on the retaining wall opposite the little taverna explained its popularity: "Welcome to Bellavista, where the Kings of Greece, the Kaiser, Tito, Nasser, Madame Sarzetaki and you have eaten." Obviously the author had been either a Socialist Royalist or an excellent PR copywriter – Madame Sarzetaki was the wife of a PASOK (Socialist) President of the Greek Republic.

Moving on, we parked below Angelokastro, the medieval fortress built to act as a look-out when marauding pirates threatened the Ionian Islands. Penny, very much in command, led us up the recently restored steps to the very top, where a little chapel had been hewn in the rock. It was here that many took refuge when the island was attacked by the Turks. Far to the east, across the island, we could make out the twin peaks of the Old Fort in Corfu Town, which, thanks to an early warning from Angelokastro, had had time to prepare for the successful defence against the Ottomans.

For our last evening we returned to Theodoros, where Fotis was on his best behaviour. I had been forgiven for past infidelity. As darkness came, Penny and I swam, Henley and Jannie watched. When the pan-fried fish arrived, we left the still warm sea. Our survey continued.

"You ask me what I would like you to do with the villa," started Penny. "Nothing really. I certainly don't need a pool; I have this glorious beach. Perhaps next time, John, you can organise a sunset. Then life would be perfect.

I turned to Henley. "Other than wine out of bottles, what do you want?"

Taking another gulp from his glass, he replied: "In fact this is excellent wine even it is served in a tin jug. Yes, my request is for Penny. Please could you find her Amerikanos and her Captain."

We laughed, had a further litre and slowly walked along the beach and up to the mountain home.

Dawn had arrived and rain had come – October often brings a week of fine weather followed by a day of rain. Swearing was coming from our guests' bedroom. They went into the sitting room from where more strong words could be heard. I got up and met them approaching down the passageway, no longer the happy couple of the night before.

Henley started. "You may only have one bathroom, but there's a shower in our room as well."

"And in the sitting room," said Penny.

"So please make our request a new roof," demanded Henley.

With our latest guests gone, we popped in to see Petros, who was, by now, desperate. He talked of getting a job in Athens. Greece was signing up to the European Fighter project and would get, in return, the opportunity to be a major maintenance contractor. He was in line for the job as Managing Director of the new company. We realised that, not only would we lose a good friend, we would have no-one to manage the renovation of the villa, if we decided to go ahead. He was one step ahead of us and introduced us to a young engineer, called Nikos, who worked for his old partner Spiros Zervos. He was a happy go lucky sort of a man in his late twenties with enough English to compensate for my lack of Greek. Well built, with blue eyes, he could have been a sportsman. We instantly liked him.

On 28 October, the day before we left, the island celebrated *Ohi Mera* – No Day. A parade was held around Corfu town to remember the day in 1940 when the dictator Metaxas had rejected Mussolini's ultimatum to occupy Greece. He had already invaded Albania in April 1939. As soon as the Italian Army crossed the Albanian border they met tough resistance from Greek troops, heroically supported by the local population, in the Pindos Mountains. The Italians were thrown back into Albania and Agii Saranda and much of the Greek-speaking south was taken. Hitler, furious at his ally's calamitous adventure, came to the rescue and swept through the Balkans to take Athens at the end of April. This diversion probably delayed, by at least a month, Operation Barbarossa, the great attack on Russia, and so may have affected the outcome of the war on the Eastern Front.

The parade was led by one of the two oldest brass bands on the island, the Kapodistrias with their black uniforms with red trim. Unlike the melancholic music they play at Easter, they struck up a fierce, happy march tune which brought the coffee drinkers on the Liston to their feet. The crowds that lined their route towards the old fort, past the podium where the President of Greece took the salute, applauded – they were proud of their history. In villages across the island there are well over twenty brass bands, known as Philharmonics, each of excellent quality. Korikiana, dressed in black with yellow epaulets, had the honour for this day. The third band was from town, the Mantzaros, whose banner boasted its origin as 1890. Between the bands marched a dozen schools, each led by a boy or girl carrying the national flag and all attired in their special uniform: waistcoats, sweaters, cardigans or jackets, single or double breasted, in navy-blue, grey-blue, cream, maroon or red; white shirts with or without ties, which were either bow, 'cowboy' or normal; short and long trousers for the boys and pleated skirts for the girls and stockings or socks always in white. Most were bare headed but some wore berets. One school was led by pupils in traditional costume. I wondered if this regimentation produced children proud of their education and void of the hooliganism which sadly is sometimes found in Britain.

As it was our final day on the island, we walked round Garitsa Bay to the taverna by the little stone mill at the southern point. There we ordered the seafood plate with its fried prawns, mussels, squid, sardines, whitebait and white fish plus marinated octopus and prawns, accompanied by delicious white Macedonian wine. The great cities of the world such as San Fransisco, Sydney and Hong Kong are on a bay. To us, Corfu Town, with the Old Fort across the water and Pantocrator in the distance, was in the same league.

Rather than take the ferry directly back to Venice, we took the Corfu-Patras leg, which was included in the standard Italy-Greece fare. As a promotion, the Strinzis Company was offering a trip to Kefalonia – for free. As it was the setting for 'Captain Corelli's Mandolin', I wanted to be Antonio returning to see Pelagia. I didn't find her. The mountains were higher than our own Pantokrator, where Corfu wanted the film to be made. Myrtou was more dramatic than anything our gorgeous west coast had to offer. But our olive green landscape scored over the barren brown of Kefalonia.

We travelled to Fiskardo in the north of the island, where the only remaining Venetian buildings stood after the terrible earthquake of 1953. There the olive groves reminded us of Corfu, but we were shocked to see the trees had been attacked by the Dakos fly. Each individual olive had a tell-tale black spot where the egg would hatch into a bug which would eat the fruit. The fly was slowly moving up through the Ionian Islands. We only hoped that those campaigning against spraying the trees in Corfu would come up with an alternative, or else the crop on the island would be badly affected.

At Christmas, we convened the family committee to decide on what we should do with Iliovasilema. I knew our daughter's love for the island and her wish that their three children and their friends could stay at the villa. The only way we could afford the renovation was to sell a flat my mother had given us in Deal. Peter, our son, had flown in, with his pregnant wife, from the Bahamas, where the beaches were better than anything we could provide in Corfu. I had assumed he would be against the sale of the flat as he was still a member of the town's magnificent golf links. When asked, he replied.

"I can always stay at a hotel in Deal, but I would never in Corfu. We will travel round the world to Agios Gordis, on one condition – if you build a swimming pool."

Louise supported her brother. Her children were keen swimmers. She, however, added her wish.

"I would like a large veranda, so I can read my books in the shade and watch the storms out to sea."

Our two children had learnt from their political father and had sewn up the vote beforehand. We therefore put Deal on the market and started designing for an upgraded home in Greece.

We had finished our market research and could now draw up our list of requirements. If our two children and their families came together, the grandparents would need an extra bedroom with an ensuite bathroom, ideally away from the rest in order to get some peace and quiet. Both families couldn't be expected to share the one minute bathroom, so we would need to provide another one as well.

Once the trees had been cut down, we would lose the shade. A veranda – perhaps the whole length of the house – would be essential. Between that and the boxes, which had been constructed as eight three-metre cubes to save the villa from following the retaining wall which had slipped seaward, we might squeeze in a swimming pool. In order to bring the machinery up the mountain and over the boxes, we must build a road, which, in time, could deliver the frail to just below the house. From there we would like a ramp for disabled access. Finally amongst all the concrete we would need jardinières for Jannie to grow her bougainvillea, jasmine, lavender, roses, wisteria, plumbago, honeysuckle and hibiscus. I would plant a Judas tree to welcome us in the spring.

On his arrival, I showed him the septic tank, the pipe and the jungle. Spiros as usual watched us from his perch above.

Taking control

Michael Pangalis's Romantic View development, across the lower road from our property, was in excellent taste. From above, it looked like a terrace of four town houses, painted pale pink, with traditional ochre-tiled roofs. Between the new buildings and the original small two-storey block, which he had bought in 1995, there was a thirteen metre pool and a huge terrace. We had enjoyed many evenings at his Romantic Palace on the beach. His wife Anna's food was superb – she came from Thrace where the Turkish influence had made her 'pots' full of wonderful flavours. Her cuisine also included mid European dishes such as goulash. Michael, a bouncy extrovert, between passionately embracing his guests, had hot feet on the dance floor. The full repertoire of Greek dancing, including carrying a table in his teeth and the fire dance, were on show each night. His troupe – his two sons and his daughter – accompanied him in the finale of his act. Our grandchildren and others would then join in to learn the steps.

I called, sometimes successfully, for the missing member of the family, Anna, to dance with her husband in a romantic rendition of the latest Greek hit. Considering the hours she spent in the kitchen, she was still remarkably beautiful. With blue eyes and light brown hair, fairer than found amongst most Greeks, she could well have had Slav blood.

However, Michael had one problem – a big one at that: Spiros. He claimed that it was Spiros's sewage that oozed under the enormous retaining wall of the road to appear on the floor of the rooms of the original building. Consequently, after any rainstorm, Michael would appear in the street and scream abuse at Spiros, who was hiding on the bridge of his ship, the equivalent of four stories above. Nikos, Spiros's son, was occasionally dispatched to view the catastrophe. Health inspectors would come but could do little to stop the feud.

Some English friends had rented a room at Michael's and they confirmed the unwelcome intrusion – black stinking sludge creeping across their room. I contacted a *News of the World* reporter whom I knew. I explained how Spiros and his German guests were destroying the holiday of the British below. I could see the headline:

GERMANS SHIT ON BRITS

I agreed to pick up a reporter and photographer from the airport. He then asked. "How many British did you say?"

"Well, only one family at the moment – the rest are Danes and Swedes."

"Forget it – the story is not big enough for us," he replied.

Michael's poolside bar was run by an energetic Montenegran and his placid Albanian sidekick, Tonassis. Having failed to solve Michael's problem, I put one to him. "I need to clear the jungle between the road and our house."

"Don't worry," he replied, "I'll get Tonassis to do it. He could do with the extra money."

Carrying Michael's tools, our new gardener arrived one afternoon just as we were leaving on an expedition. On our return, the jungle, now ten feet tall, remained untouched. It seemed that Spiros had shouted at Tonassis. No one knew why, but Tonassis had run for his life.

At this point, Michael's neighbour, an ex-policeman we called PC Poulis, arrived. He was a very unhappy man. As he didn't speak English, our conversation was limited by my inadequate Greek. He pointed to the jungle.

"*Megalo problima.*"

I explained, mainly in sign language, that the 'big problem' would soon be solved. Michael's Albanian was going to clear the land. I had obviously misunderstood him.

"*Eki pera – prasinos solinas!*"

Lesson Three from my Greek studies thirty years before came flooding back – the *"Eki pera. Pas eki tora."* Over there was something green. I looked at the jungle – it was all green. Slightly confused I looked again and then I saw it. Hidden in the brambles was what I thought, at first glance, was a huge green snake. On further inspection I realised he was referring to a thick green reinforced plastic pipe.

He then pointed to Spiros's septic tank and the pipe again. The penny dropped. *Spiros was pumping his sewage onto my land.* No wonder the jungle had grown so well. I now knew why Spiros didn't want Tonassis to cut down the jungle and reveal his secret.

I went down to see my friendly councillor, Spiros 'Mini-market' Mazis, who had been elected the previous year. He had received most votes for Sinarades council and was therefore the village's representative on the district council as well. He was a useful man to know.

"Spiros has been pumping sewage on my land," I complained.

"Yes, I know – *and also into your neighbour's abandoned well.*"

I was shocked. My land was bad enough, but a well was going too far. "What can I do to stop him?" I asked.

"But Spiros says you gave him permission!"

"Well, I haven't," I replied.

"Get yourself a lawyer, John," he recommended.

Elena suggested we talked to her son, Tony. In the old days he had windsurfed for Greece in the World Championships. Tall and fabulously built he was a sensation on a board. Now he had tried his hand at golf. It wasn't a success. The one time I had played with him that year, it had taken four hours to get round. Before every shot we took, we had to wait for those ahead of us. It was a hot day. As my irritation increased, I became hotter still. Tony removed his shirt and played bare chested.

"Tony, you saw the message on the first tee? It said: 'Shirts must be worn'."

"What can they do about it?" replied Tony. "Anyway, it's my island."

He had a point. At my championship course in England, he would have been barred for indecent conduct. In Corfu, they wouldn't expel anyone, as there were only thirty-five local members. Perhaps golf didn't suit the Greek character. Though I had great faith in the island's future, and the golf course was excellently designed even if slightly lacking in maintenance, we would definitely not be competing with the Algarve or Spain. I was rather happy about that. Visitors to Corfu should come for nature's offerings: the countryside, the villages, the beaches and, above all, the locals.

Tony, however, was only too happy to introduce us to his lawyer, Costas Tsivanides, of the legal firm, Socrates Konstantinos Tsivanides. Costas was supercharged. He spoke fast in perfect English. Of course he would help, but first he wanted to visit the villa.

On his arrival, I showed him the septic tank, the pipe and the jungle. Spiros as usual watched us from his perch above. We climbed up to the house and sat under our great olive tree. He noted Spiros had concreted the terrace and built a jardinière in front it.

"He's running your property, isn't he?"

"Yes," I replied meekly. "We drew up an agreement whereby he uses the villa in July and the first half of August. In return he maintains the property. He also pays the electricity and, until last year, pumped water into my gravity tank. He also uses my *sterna*, the rainwater storage tank, as his own."

We went to investigate the electricity meter.

"It's right next to his stairs," said Costas. "The electricity is going directly into his building. Anyway, what proof do you have that the meter is on your land – you don't have a boundary fence."

"Well, I did, but he covered it when he built the apartments. He offered to buy some land from us, but I refused and demanded he make us a garage in compensation. He then built only a drive-in, which I now find is over his septic tank."

We returned to analyse our findings.

"First, if you are right and the meter is on your land, his building is illegal. It must be five metres from the boundary – it isn't. So how did he get a permit? Perhaps he didn't. In Greece, we have an excellent arrangement that a developer cannot get electricity until the authority have confirmed that the building conforms to the plans. Maybe Spiros didn't need electricity – he had yours."

My argument with Spiros had been over the sewage. Costas had now extended it. He seemed to be gathering further ammunition to flatten Spiros.

"I will summon Spiros to my office and tell him that you are restoring your electricity, that he must desist from pouring sewage on your land and that you will be erecting a fence along the boundary. Basically, if he plays ball, we won't discuss the legality of his building. But first we must first ensure that you are legal. If your tax is not paid up to date, you don't have a leg to stand on if this dispute goes to court."

We had a substantial backlog of tax to pay. So every evening Jannie and I would go in to town and get the maximum from the cash machine. With this we started to drip feed our accountant, who paid money, on account, to the tax man and negotiated the total down until it was less than the money we could get out of the wall. We reported to Costas that now we were 'legal'.

A couple of days later, Costas told us that Spiros hadn't turned up to their meeting, but would be sending his lawyer. The next time we met, we heard that the two lawyers had met. Spiros's lawyer had agreed with Costas that I was in the right, whereupon Spiros sacked him.

"I've now told Spiros that we will cut off the electricity at the end of September and he must get his own. You must also put the fence up."

Petros, now back from Athens, was happy to get involved again, and asked his old friend Kontos to erect the fence. He was told that he would find the old fence under the ground and put the new one on top.

Kontos arrived. Spiros shouted. Kontos left.

Our next visit to Costas showed why it is essential to have a good lawyer in Greece. He explained what he had done. "I've drawn up an agreement: no more argument about the fence, remove his pipes and you will let him disconnect the electricity at the end of the season. I've told him unless he agrees; I will question his original planning permission. I am sure he will sign."

Returning home we found Spiros's son Nikos waiting for us.

"Why are you causing problems for my father?" he asked. "He has looked after your house for many years."

"And poured sewage on my land," I replied.

"He says he won't do that again. Why do you want to put the fence up? You are only here a few weeks each year."

"Tell your father, we are going to live here for at least four months each year. Tell him that in future he cannot let the house out."

Nikos was shaken.

"But I stay here when my father's place is full," he said.

I now knew why he was so unhappy.

"Just tell him he will have to sign the agreement or else I will cut off his electricity next week."

"But it will cost a lot of money and will take time. We have guests and they need electricity," replied Nikos.

We heard a few hours later that Spiros had phoned Costas and agreed to sign. I reckoned he was more worried about Costas's threat than mine. I could understand the timing problem, but wondered why it would cost him so much. I could only surmise what the authorities had said and how he got his supply.

As Petros Kardakis and our new engineer Nikos were in the same office block as Costas, we often walked by to check if they were in. With the town now a solid traffic jam, the professionals had resorted to travel by two wheels. Nikos used a battered little Honda moped while Costas had a classic vintage tourer – an early Japanese version of a Harley Davidson. It told a lot about their characters.

Kontos came back and put the fence up. Spiros claimed that the boundary was at my side of my drive in (and his septic tank), while I considered it was on his side. We agreed on splitting it right down the middle, which could have interesting repercussions in the future.

We could now start renovating the house with the replacement of the windows and French doors, which were rotten and partially eaten by termites. We installed plastic covered-aluminium units made to measure. They were double glazed with dark green shutters – the Venetian colour uniquely found in Corfu and the other Ionian Islands. Elsewhere in Greece windows were dark blue and walls white. Between the shutters and its French door we had a pull-down mosquito net – days of being bitten to pieces were over.

In a further attempt to be legal, we visited the district office which dealt with water bills. As we hadn't paid anything for eighteen months, we were referred to the overdue section in town. As we had no papers and no address, we had a problem. 'Waller' and 'Iliovasilema' failed to locate the entry on his ledger. At last he found us.

"*Englesos, Sinarades*?" he queried. Our new name was 'Englishman, Sinarades', expressed in a rather colloquial way.

Our next challenge was to clear the jungle. Michael's man had failed; so we decided to look for a gardener. Corfu has an excellent monthly English Newspaper – *The Corfiot*. It has a lot of useful information, which is repeated from month to month: lists of property for sale and rent, bus timetables, details of restaurants and adverts for services wanted and provided. We read: "Gardens maintained, grass cut, trees trimmed, etc. Own equipment – lawn mower, chain saw etc, call Fred."

This was exactly what we were looking for; so we phoned Fred.

"We have a jungle to clear," I explained.

"Don't worry! Fred will clear anything," he said.

Next day, a small bearded, balding man of my age, arrived in his little Fiat with a trailer attached. He looked at the brambles and concluded, in a North American accent, "That's not a problem."

I wondered what was.

"I only have one rule," he added, "I don't work in the rain."

We agreed a price to clear the land and burn the rubbish. I was impressed with our Canadian. It reminded me of what the Canadians call their nuclear power plant: CANDU.

Fred spent our last Saturday in the jungle. I didn't envy him. He used a petrol-driven strimmer with a metal blade rather than the usual plastic cord. In four hours, less a break for a "couple of cold ones", he hacked his way along the route of the pipe. The main part crossed our land. In the olive grove next door, where the undergrowth had also grown to fearsome proportions, we found another pipe – the spur that took the sewage into our neighbour's well.

Before we left for England, Petros came over. Sitting under the olive tree – its great boughs and branches stretching nine metres over the terrace – he ate a little, talked a lot and drank non-stop. The years seemed to slip off his burdened shoulders as we told him what we wanted to do. However hard life was, the engineer was happy tackling the technical issues.

Nearly thirty years before, we had sat in the same spot and planned our future home. We had wanted to build a Scandinavian summer house which would nestle in the olive groves. Because of lack of money, the villa couldn't have a veranda – an essential ingredient of its northern cousin. Nature, in the form of our great olive tree, would provide shade from the midday sun.

Now, Jannie and I wanted to extend our house. "Do you remember your visit to Denmark to see Jannie's brother? You told me you saw a development of 'L' shaped single-storied houses. Each house was totally secluded from its neighbour but each had a beautiful view. We want the same here."

Petros laughed. "They were designed by Jørn Utzon, the architect of the Sydney Opera House – and you want the same?"

"Well, our idea is to add a wing at the north end to make our house L-shaped. It would contain a bedroom and two bathrooms," I suggested. "With a veranda the length of the present building connected to another one in front of the extension, we would have cloisters." We looked along the house to the far end where the annexe would jut out. Spiros was on his bridge checking up on what we were doing. "Being nine metres long, it would totally block his view of our living area. He could no longer see us," I argued with enthusiasm.

"The cost would be very high because you would need to put the building on stilts," said Petros.

I was saddened. "Can we at least extend the house at the far end and then have a veranda and pool in front?" I asked.

"Of course, and better still I will get you the best prefabricated pool from Athens – maybe the one which is eight metres long and four metres wide."

Before Petros left, we got up and made for our jungle, beyond and below which we could barely see the main road.

"Petros, with the grandchildren happy – they are getting their pool – can you satisfy the old folk as well?" I asked.

"We will want a road up the property so that we will no longer need to climb the steps."

"Do you remember what the Athenian engineer said when the retaining wall slipped? There are three ways of holding up a mountain: you can build walls, plant trees or, if you are lucky, have large boulders in the ground. With slippery clay under the topsoil, you have few boulders. So he constructed some boulders for you, really big ones – the eight boxes. You will face the same problem when you build the road – how do you stop it from sliding down the mountain?" he asked.

"Don't tell me, I'll build some more boxes," I replied, giggling in my slightly inebriated state.

"Well, we have two options," said Petros. "We could raise a high retaining wall from the edge of the main road. This is the Corfiot solution. Just look at the Pink Palace. But your olive trees would be buried under the rising road and you will create a blot on the landscape. Alternatively, we could leave the olive trees, which already hold up the land, and build the road diagonally across the property, raising it up to the level we are on now, by making a box or two on its corner below the present boxes. Under the jungle, there is still the steep track which the bulldozer made when it climbed up to construct the original boxes. This has settled over the years and could be the base of your new road. Don't build walls along the road as these might slide – just leave the surface to settle and slip if it wants to."

As we said goodbye, I promised that I would draw up some plans on my return to England, which he would discuss with Nikos, the new young engineer.

On our last evening, we packed ready to go and went in to check with Costas, our lawyer, that Spiros had signed the agreement. He hadn't. It felt like being two-one down going into injury time. He still had his electricity and his pipe, which he would connect up to his septic tank as soon as we left. We had our fence.

In the middle of the night, while Jannie slept, I put on some old clothes and my working boots and crept out down to the jungle. In the light of the moon, I found the main pipe and started to pull. It started to move. By some superhuman effort I tugged the thirty metre snake out, heaved it up the road and left it in front of Belvedere Apartments. Torn but victorious, I returned to bed. We left to catch the seven o'clock ferry to Venice well before it was light. Jannie was not amused.

"You shouldn't have done that – he'll get his own back," she said.

Back in England, serious design started. I tried different solutions and finished up with the simplest, which I turned into plans and elevations on my PC. The heart of our new 'home' would be a veranda right across the front of the old house. It would access all the rooms through French windows. All year round we would use it as a huge open air living room, with the dining area in front of the kitchen. To close off the veranda at the north, Spiros's end, we would add a double bedroom with its own bathroom and another en-suite to the existing main bedroom. These would be extensions of the present house.

Looking out from the veranda, we would have a panoramic view of the sea with a pool just in front. On the right would be the pool terrace with a pergola, beside the annexe. Perhaps a honeysuckle could be planted next to its window – to remind us of our gorgeously scented room by the harbour in Benitses, where we stayed on our first visit to the island.

At the left end of the veranda, we would have steps descending to a lower terrace where our new road would end. My own personal requirement could be met. Many of Corfu's older village houses had a covered first floor landing, known as a *bodzo*, accessed from below by stone stairs. By stretching the imagination, we would also have a *bodzo*.

Around the lower terrace would be traditional stone walls and Jannie's jardinières.

When it was all finished we would have a real home. In the morning, when the sun peeped over the mountain at ten o'clock, we would have breakfast on the pool terrace under the pergola. With the sun at its zenith, we would have lunch under the shade of the veranda. In the evening, we would sit on the olive tree terrace and watch the sun go down through the leaves of the tree and dine out until the moon came over the mountain to tell us it was bedtime.

We came back in mid March 2001. The ferry arrived late in the evening so we spent our first night in the Hotel Kavalieri on the Esplanade. Opening the window in the morning to a crisp sun, with the snow covered mountains on the mainland in the distance, the passion we felt for Corfu was awoken. In trepidation, we drove out to Sinarades and down the mountain road to the villa. Over the winter, there had been many rock falls which would be cleared before the tourists arrived at the end of April.

As usual, we parked below the house. We gasped. Fred had cleared the jungle to reveal the original olive trees and our little home, poking its head above the trees. We entered the house and the lights didn't switch on. For the first time in Corfu, we were excited by the lack of electricity. Spiros had cut the supply as he had promised – he now had his own. Our first priority was to reconnect ourselves.

Returning to town, we immediately sought out Petros, who had just finished packing all his files and vacating his office. His news was wonderful. He had landed a fantastic job as the senior engineer on the project to construct the Olympic Village, with a team of sixty working for him. He had passed on my plans to Nikos with some of his own ideas.

Along the corridor next to Spiros Zervos, Petros's old partner, was a small room with a long table deep in plans and paperwork. Sitting at a computer was Nikos. Instantly one recognised a weakness and a strength. Unlike Petros, he was disorganised. However, he was up-to-date technically. He greeted us and immediately printed out 3-D images of our new villa. His new toy was brilliant.

At that moment, a very slim, extremely pretty late twenty-year-old came in.

"I'm Anna, Nikos's wife," she said in excellent English.

"And my interpreter at times," he laughed. In fact his English was perfectly adequate although some words always came out wrong, such as 'style' for 'steel'.

"What do you think of our plans?" she asked.

I was thrilled to discover that we had a husband and wife team. She was an architect and he was an engineer. "Brilliant," I replied, referring perhaps to the software as well as the design. It had converted my simple solution into a real building.

"We are not certain yet how the roof will look on the new building," Anna said. This was their name for the annexe. She produced some sketches she had made. I decided we had an artist as well in the team.

The one big discrepancy from my original ideas was that the veranda, for half its length, would be a pergola. It could be a major problem. One can look up through a pergola. That was fine. But Spiros could look down on us. We agreed that we should meet at Iliovasilema next day for a light lunch and some serious talking.

Nikos and Anna drove up in his BMW – it fitted his image. Anna was excited by the location. "When the trees have gone you will need the veranda for the shade," she said. Turning to Jannie, she asked. "Wouldn't it be wonderful having a bougainvillea climbing up over the pergola?"

Shamefully, I wasn't going to let anyone else put their case. "Nikos, as an engineer, you always find out what the problem is before coming up with a solution?"

"Yes," he replied, uncertain of where I was going.

"I have three problems, which I want you to fix."

"OK." He was interested – I thought he liked solving problems.

"The problems are Spiros, Spiros and Spiros. The solutions are privacy, privacy, privacy. I am NOT having my neighbour spy on me. I am NOT having a pergola. We will have a veranda along the whole length of the house."

They looked up at Spiros. Sure enough, there he was, on his bridge, watching us – he wanted to know what was going on. We hid around the house under the olive tree and Jannie brought the food out. As time went on, we learnt that Nikos did not drink alcohol during the working day. He made an exception on that day as he was celebrating a new contract.

"I've brought you a bottle of my own wine," he said. I checked the pretty label with a picture on it: 'Lefkimmi 1999, Nikos Papavlassopoulos.'

"Our area makes the best wine on the island, so I hope you like it." I opened it and we agreed it was delicious. "I print all the labels on the computer," he said proudly. "I give my friends a bottle for Christmas. When they meet up at night they drink it – it becomes like any other wine. This Christmas I had a brilliant idea. I changed the program to add a personalised message: 'Produced especially for .....' and it inserted the name of my friend. Now they keep the wine as it has a unique value. Next year, I'll have a bottle 'for John and Jannie'."

A few days later, we saw their latest plans. Nikos, the engineer, had rejected all Anna's sketches for the roof. "I have continued the line of the present roof over the new building. It will be easier to construct," he explained. I was happy. I liked the old roof, so I knew I would like the new one.

"How long will it take to get planning permission?" I asked.

"Between three months and a year," he replied, "but I hope we can do it quickly."

"I hope so as well. Our son, Peter, and his family are coming from the Bahamas at the beginning of September. It is essential that the work is finished by then."

"I cannot guarantee anything, John, but we'll do our best."

"You have to do a lot of paper work – how much will your fee be?"

"As you are Petros's friend, I will charge you the minimum." It sounded too good. But there was a catch. "Remember, during the building phase, I don't want to spend all my time supervising the workers," he added. "You must find yourself your own builder."

Reluctantly, I agreed. Then he explained that we needed to get a permit before he could connect our electricity supply.

We drove to Alepou and joined the queue at the Electricity Board. Eventually it was our turn. I explained our problem.

"Have you an old bill?" the clerk asked.

"No."

"Then how do I know you ever had electricity?"

I gave her our meter number. She checked on her computer.

"Mr. Grammenos pays the bills. It's not yours."

"Can I have a new permit please?" I asked.

"Of course," she replied, now certain that I never had electricity and I had been lying all the time. She produced a list of all the documents we had to obtain: wiring diagram, application form, proof of land ownership, planning permission, identity papers, even a statement from the police that we were nice people.

Nikos filled in the application form and had the standard letter for the police typed. We waited in a queue at the police station and watched an elderly couple shouting at each other. The duty officer eventually turned up and removed the man but the woman continued to pour out abuse. At long last, we produced our passports and the letter, which he read. He removed a tin from a drawer in his ancient metal desk. It contained the coins which he collected, the stamps he stuck on forms and the rubber imprints he inked and pressed on letters. Finally, with a flourish, he confirmed we were law abiding citizens. He didn't know who we were and probably didn't care. He was bored by paperwork and fighting families and would have preferred driving round town, between traffic jams, in his police car. On the other hand, for a couple of coins, we had been entertained for an hour and received another piece of paper. As it was after 1.30 we deferred a second visit to the Electricity Board: they were closed.

Next day we returned, queued, presented our documents and were told we must go to the local Council. It would confirm that our original planning permit was up-to-date, there had been no new development and we still owned the land. A few days later we had our electricity.

Finding a builder was easier. We saw a pre-mixed concrete lorry at George Texaco. Ankle deep in concrete, a Wellington boot-wearing mini-man was slamming a plank edgeways onto the surface to smooth it down. From head to toe, he was speckled grey with spilt concrete. George introduced us. His name was Zacharias. He was short and slightly built, unlike most Greek workmen, who looked as if they could be wrestlers or weight lifters in their spare time. His physique was less a result of under nourishment and abstinence – we were sure he ate ample meat and drank plenty of wine – but excess of energy. George told him that he was now working for us as well and would get the same money per cubic metre of concrete poured. He said he would meet our engineer in the afternoon at our house.

I phoned Nikos from George's office. He was pleased with my initiative.

"Have you got yourself a bulldozer driver as well?" he asked.

"No. Doesn't the builder do everything?" I countered.

"Of course not. Your man only does the concrete walls."

I turned to George. "You wouldn't know a good bulldozer driver?" I asked.

"Sure, meet Nikos."

George's office was always full of customers and workmen. The coffee machine was doing a roaring business – particularly as the drinks were free. It served the purpose of the traditional cafenion in the village – the hub of the area's intelligence network – where gossip was exchanged and deals were done. Even the backgammon board was brought out when business was slow.

Nikos, who turned out to be another Grammenos, was not related to the other Grammenoses – the three Georges and the two Spiros. He was a middleweight in his late twenties with dark eyes.

"What can I do for you?" he asked in very passable English.

"We are building a road up to our house. Can you help?"

"No problem."

He agreed to attend the site meeting. We left.

"We now have two Nikos," said Jannie. "What shall we call them?"

"Papavlassopoulos is a mouthful. As he is the engineer he'll be Nikos Mechanikos. The other will be Nikos Bulldozer – it's the same word in Greek."

The town team, Nikos Mechanikos plus Petros's partner, Spiros, arrived on time. Moments later 'Little and Large', our local wall builder and bulldozer driver, turned up. Zacharias was almost unrecognisable. He was in his jacket and smart trousers and wore polished leather city shoes instead of boots.

Nikos Mechanikos, from the bottom of the stairs, pointed up to the right where the track, which the bulldozer had made when we built the boxes so many years ago, was still visible. "The road goes up, across the property, to that olive tree." We walked up. "We will here make a ten metre long corner wall, rising up to the old boxes," he continued.

"*Megalo problima*," said Zacharias and continued, like a machine gun, to expand on his problem. The two engineers joined in.

I turned to Nikos Bulldozer. "Can you do what Nikos wants?"

"No problem. But Zacharias says the new wall will slide down the mountain just as your original retaining wall did thirty years ago."

"What's he saying then?" I asked him.

"We must build a thirty metre wall next to the main road, rising to eight metres high, and a fifteen metre wall up the boundary. This is what he did at the Pink Palace," said Nikos Bulldozer.

The mention of 'Pink Palace' was like a red rag to a bull. Spiros 'Pink Palace' Grammenos had turned a green hillside into a concrete monolith. I still had olive trees, broom and a mass of wild flowers next to the road. They held up the land and they were beautiful. Why would anyone want to create yet another eyesore? I already had one next door. It then dawned on me. Our builder had a vested interest. He liked building huge walls – the bigger the better. It made him more money.

Mental arithmetic was a valuable asset in Greece. I calculated that Zacharias wanted to build walls with a surface of 200 square metres while Nikos's version would be 30.

The argument increased in volume. Arms were waved frantically. My mind went into overdrive. I could see my £2,000 road becoming £20,000.

"John, what do you think?" asked Spiros Zervos, Petros's partner. In the end it would be my responsibility.

"I agree with Nikos. When Petros was here, he suggested we build the wall on the corner and leave the road across the property to settle, slip and stabilise and then surface it later." I turned to Nikos. "Tell Zacharias that if he builds our wall well, we will need him to construct a larger wall, twenty metres long, in front of the house."

Suddenly the angry wasp became the happy butterfly. We had reached a typical Greek compromise. Everyone was satisfied. I would get my small wall. He would build two walls instead of one and therefore pour more concrete. I just hoped my cheapskate approach wouldn't cause problems in the future.

It was agreed that the work would start once we had planning permission, which Nikos explained was being applied for any day. He then asked Zacharias to measure the height of the proposed road above the main road. He needed it for the planning application. There was a maximum slope we could have for a road.

The following afternoon, Zacharias returned, in his smart outfit, with an assistant. He asked for a bottle of water – I assumed he was thirsty. He rejected my unopened litre and a half of Zagori mineral water and indicated tap water was OK. I duly obliged. Instead of drinking it he poured it into a thin tube some fifteen metres long. Mystified I watched him hand one end to his mate, while he took the other end and started to climb an olive tree below the track. Experience had taught me that one needed two hands and proper boots to scale a tree. Zacharias had one free hand and wore his slippery city shoes – but up he went like a squirrel. He stopped when he was at the same height as his mate up the hill. Then with much shouting they adjusted the ends of the pipe until the water levels were the same. With a measure Zacharias worked out the distance to the ground and then descended. Numbers were being called and Zacharias was computing furiously. He then fought his way through the uncleared jungle just above the main road and climbed another olive tree.

Having watched this performance, I walked down the fifty-four steps from where Zacharias's mate was standing to the road. At 19 centimetres each I had descended about ten metres.

Zacharias, now on the road, announced. *"Deka metra."*

We agreed but I didn't say anything as he was the expert. To double check he repeated the exercise by climbing up different olive trees. As an exhibition of youthful agility, his method was the clear winner. However, I wondered why he didn't use his system and measure down the steps instead of up the olive trees. With running water and electricity installed, we had just one amenity missing – the telephone. Mobiles were useless as the mountain totally cut off reception. The single call box in the valley was used by all the tourists. As luck would have it, new telephone poles were being erected along the road; we had just had one installed at the bottom of the property. By constant pressure I had a line hung from the pole to our house, through the wall, and into the sitting room. I gave the line installer the phone we had purchased from his head office.

"That's not my job. Another man will come and connect the telephone."

I now faced another battle with the bureaucracy to get the new man to come. "When will he come?" I asked our line man.

"*Avrio i methavrio* – tomorrow or the day after."

Next day I phoned the office and asked if he was coming.

"*Avrio*," they replied.

The following day I phoned again.

"*Avrio*," they replied again.

"But the installer had said '*Avrio i methavrio*'. Today is *methavrio*." I had learnt a new trick - it seemed that *methavrio* had a definitive meaning. He came, and we were connected to the outside world.

April had a special attraction – the buzz of a new year: houses were painted; fences were fixed; stone terraces were swept; and furniture was put out ready for the tourists. The first of the itinerant traders arrived.

"*Karekles, trapezakia – ola plastika*," we would hear as the overloaded open lorry crept down the mountain to the valley – "chairs, small tables, everything plastic". If I was quick enough, I could get down the steps before the lorry had rounded the hairpin bend.

"*Gourounia*" was a new call, so I ran down to the road below where the lorry had stopped. The father was driving and calling out "pigs" while his two boys were in the back with the animals. One of them, a born salesman, produced a squealing piglet and offered it to me. By chance, I was holding our camera. He was a born actor. He held the wriggling baby to his face. I swear they were both grinning from ear to ear.

Summer would bring the little van with the cry of "*psaria freska, eho psaria*," – "fresh fish, I have fish." In the autumn, a swaying house on wheels would pass to the message of "*galopoula*," – "turkeys." Locals would buy these and fatten them up for Christmas.

Our final task before returning home was to cut down the remaining poplars just in front of the house and the olive tree where the corner of the road would be built. Fred performed brilliantly – his chain saw was smoking from continuous use. The result was literally an eye-opener. The view to Ortholithi, the 'erect rock' island, was restored; we could now see the sunset as it turned the whole horizon ablaze; but above all we could stare in awe at the double sun – one falling slowly as the afternoon went on and the other reflected in a sparkling sea.

With the land clear, we awaited the conclusion of Nikos's battle with the bureaucracy in the town hall. It left one little job. Above the house was an enormous water tank which was connected to the Pink Palace down the road by five thick rubber pipes. They passed over our land and had to be removed before our bulldozer arrived. Spiros 'Pink Palace' Grammenos's son, Dr. George, promised to move them into the olive groves next door.

"Don't worry. I will remove them *avrio*," he said.

Within an hour, Nikos has reached the top and comes down again smoothing all the way. I now have a perfect road. He goes up to the top again and digs out a trench with three steps: the base for the concrete box on the corner, where the wooden frame will sit.

PART TWO – CONSTRUCTION

Excavating the mountain

We return to Corfu on 13 June with a mammoth task ahead. In the early hours of 9 September, our son Peter and his family will arrive from the Bahamas. By then, we must have built the road up the mountain, so we can get machinery up to make the swimming pool with a terrace around it. We will put a new roof on the house, erect a veranda and start on the extension which will contain a bedroom and two bathrooms. As we must be in England during August, we have less than seven weeks to complete the major part of the work. Knowing Greek workers, we can expect little to be done when we are away. Even more worrying is that when I phoned from Venice, before catching the ferry, I was told that we still haven't received planning permission.

Thursday 14 June 2001, 47 days to go

We arrived last night. This morning promises a glorious day. The sun remains hidden by the mountains above the house to the east. To the west, some 100 metres below, is the open expanse of the Mediterranean, dead calm at this time of day. To the south is glorious Corfu in its virgin state: endless terraces of olive groves majestically stepping down the mountain of Garouna towards the little village of Pentati and the sea below, on which glides Ortholithi. Literally translated as the 'erect rock', the hundred foot island is the symbol of our beautiful beach.

My first job is to check that George 'Pink Palace' Grammenos has moved his water pipes from my land where the bulldozer will be constructing the road. Not surprisingly, the pipes are still there, just as they were six weeks ago, when he promised to move them to the empty olive grove next door.

"*Avrio!*" he had said. Tomorrow!

I go ballistic. Nobody, but nobody, is going to delay the project. If he won't remove them I'll just cut them and throw them next door. I creep out of the house because Jannie knows about my temper and would undoubtedly try and calm me down. I follow the water pipes down the hill to the Pink Palace Hotel, where hundreds of guests will soon be in for a very dry summer if I do cut the pipes.

"No, Dr George is not here - he's asleep," I'm told.

"Give me some paper," I demand, and then scribble a message to the Doctor (Doctor of what nobody seems to know): "REMOVE PIPES TODAY OR I CUT THEM".

I make a rapid exit as I have no wish to meet Dr. George's father, Spiros 'Pink Palace' Grammenos. In the 70s, he used to invite me into what was then little more than a disco-bar by shouting "Beer, Capitalist." To a man who had started with nothing, a young foreigner with ready cash must surely have seemed very rich.

Now it is Spiros, with his vast hotel, who is the capitalist.

I return home for the next battle and phone Nikos 'Mechanikos' to check on the planning approval.

"The architects didn't meet yesterday, but they will meet today," he assures me. "We will also need a document from Parelion," he adds, referring to our local *dimos* – council. "My contact there, Sophia Kotsibou, says it's being prepared. Can you go and see if it's ready?"

The Parelion community offices are in the Ropa Valley, at the centre of the five villages it administers. On the way, we pass George 'Texaco' Grammenos. He is all smiles. On the forecourt is Nikos 'Bulldozer' Grammenos and a large hole.

This is where George is building a pair of huge underground tanks for the car wash he is going to buy.

Out comes a very little man, wizened by working out-of-doors, but handsome in a mischievous way. I immediately recognise him as Zacharias, the wall builder we had agreed to do our work, when we left in April. Same size, same age, same looks, but he is not Zacharias. George explains that Pavlos is his brother. Zacharias is working on a big project in Paxos and will be away for a month.

George discusses my problems with Pavlos, who is only too willing to get another job, although probably he has a few others going on at the same time. Everyone is building in Corfu, even if it is only shells of future homes. It seems that the brothers are no longer working together, so Pavlos will phone Zacharias and check that it's OK and find out the price he can get from the Englishman, I reckon.

I pre-empt him. "13,000 drachmas (£26) a cubic metre, OK?"

"OK."

"When can you start?"

"Tuesday or Wednesday," he replies.

We exchange telephone numbers and agree to meet next day.

Caroline, George's delightful English wife, appears. She welcomes us back. So I ask her what Pavlos is like.

"Alright - he's here today, though he was meant to be here the day before yesterday."

I ignore the warning; at least we have a builder. As we leave, I ask Jannie. "Why are wall builders so small?"

She doesn't know – well nor do I – but I suggest that it's because they have to build concrete tanks. This entails pouring concrete on the base of a hole dug by the bulldozer, then making a wooden frame for the walls and a wooden roof with a whole in it. They fill up the wall cavities with concrete and then pour concrete on the roof. At that point the small man wins as he is the one who can get into the box to remove the wooden frame. We agree Pavlos passes the size test.

We drive down the hill and around the road we call the Sinarades bypass. We never drive into the village; it is too old and peaceful for cars. Along the bypass, we observe one of the island's biggest problems, rubbish. In the old days every discarded plastic bottle or plastic bag was left on the side of the road. Nowadays, there are wheelie bins all round the island and household waste no longer despoils the landscape. However, there is still nowhere for builders to take their rubble, old timbers, fridges, stoves and other refuse. They just tip it beside the road on the outskirts of their village. After a while, a bulldozer pushes the pile into the undergrowth and a sign is put up - no tipping. The builders then find another site.

After the bypass, we drive north. Ahead of us is the almost Tuscan sight of the village of Pelekas standing shining white on top of a hill. We pass the local vineyards, producing some of the most drinkable wine on the island. *Kakotrigis*, meaning "difficult to pick", is called white but is really yellow. Looking like Vin Jaune from the Jura, it has a powerful taste and is certainly not something to overindulge in. The red wine is from the *Petrokorintho* grape, a match for any Chateauneuf-du-Pape. Sadly very little is produced and it is almost impossible to find unless it has been blended with its white brother. My friends describe it as 'interesting', 'slightly sweet at first then becoming drier as it's drunk' and 'very quaffable'. Put a litre of *Petrokorintho* and a bottle of St. Emilion on the table at dinner and both are downed with pleasure; but it is the Greek wine that's more popular than the French at the end.

Our road crosses the road from Pelekas to Town. Here Vassilis and Eleni have just opened the 'Crossroads Taverna'. This lovely couple have moved from their kebab café, 'Fast Food Vassilis', which they rented in the village, to their own place in which they said they would produce the most wonderful Greek cuisine, "only from fresh ingredients". We promise ourselves an early visit. We go on past the olive groves on the left, covered in the spring with honesty, more blue in Corfu than in England, and the prolific pink cranesbill. As all the flowers are now dead and the land is dry, we will have to wait to September for colour, when the minute cyclamen appear, crowding in their mauve outfit on every bank and in every dell.

Finally, we come to the Ropa Valley, and turn right towards the little community offices, where the Council officers are out in force, marking the road. Parelion confirms that we are back in Greece – nothing is ready. Spiros, a Council officer, who speaks English, checks with Sophia. "It's a pity Nikos didn't ask earlier," says Sophia. "We had a meeting last week. The next one is at the end of the month."

From my seventeen years on Richmond Council, the penny drops. It is time to find a councillor. Another Brit is waiting in the office.

"We've just bought an old house and our engineer tells us it will only take a few days to get planning permission to build an extension," he says.

I smile wisely but say nothing and leave him waiting. We go into town to tell Nikos the good news, the builder, and the bad news, the paper. Nikos's news was not good either.

"They cancelled today's meeting as one of the architects had to go to a funeral, but they will definitely meet next Tuesday."

Our day ends on a high note, two chicken plates at George "Georgy Porgy" Grammenos in the village. It makes us forget problems with permits. His wife Labrini is all smiles. With her electric carver, she elegantly removes succulent pieces of lamb from the *giros* or doner. We order a plate; it's delicious. Unwisely we accept a second half-litre of his lethal blend of local wines.

Friday 15 June, 2 down and 45 to go

I'm woken by two men outside. It seems Dr. George has sent them up to sort out the problem of the pipes.

"Dr. George, good man. Dr. George very angry you say you cut his pipes."

Instead of digging the pipes out of the branches and undergrowth, the workmen turn off each of the five pipes, unscrew a connection by the road, pull out the pipe, throw it next door and then reconnect the pipe. Within an hour the work is finished. If it had been done in March, we would still all be friends. So I go down to the Pink Palace to write another note thanking Dr. George. This time I don't ask to see him.

On the way back, I discuss my work plans with Spiros 'Mini-Market' Mazis, the new councillor for Sinarades. He seems rather laid back about the permit, but advises me to get agreement from my neighbours before doing any work. Michael who owns the Romantic View Hotel below won't be a problem as he's a friend. Spiros on the right might not be either as he is now trying to build bridges with his "good morning Mr. Wallace" routine. That leaves our neighbour on the left, who owns the olive grove and the disused well into which Spiros directed his sewage. He is the previous owner of "*O Yiannis*" in Anemomilos. We now have another good reason to visit the most wonderful "pot" restaurant on the island, to find out where we could contact him.

At 3 p.m., everyone arrives to plan the project. It is remarkable how they all turn up at the same time, but I think Nikos Bulldozer and Pavlos met at George Texaco and waited until Nikos Mechanikos drove past. Perhaps more surprising is that everyone is on time, but this is the *first* meeting.

Nikos Mechanikos repeats to Pavlos what he told Zacharias in the spring: that the road will cross the mountain and we will build a corner wall to hold up the road as it turns onto a terrace in front of the house, where we will build the pool. We will allow the rest of the road down to the entrance to settle for a year and then we might build a retaining wall before giving it a concrete surface.

Pavlos is unhappy. He has obviously been talking to his brother, who had proposed a retaining wall along the whole length of the main road and then up the boundary. Our plan will save millions of drachmas, which is not in Pavlos's interest. Nikos concedes that the corner wall could become a box, as I like boxes not walls. None of the original boxes we built thirty years ago has slipped. A box, with four sides instead of the two of the corner box will need double the concrete, so Pavlos also likes the idea.

We then discuss the S-word, sewage, not Spiros's from next door, which had fertilised our jungle for so many years, but our own. Now that the house will be lived in for much of the year we need a proper solution to our sanitary problems. The original soakaway has become lost in the jungle. Now we talk of a real septic tank. Pavlos's eyes brighten up. As an expert tank builder, he can see that even my small one will bring in more money.

We move up to the house to discuss the pool. Pavlos doesn't like my idea of a pre-fabricated pool: it is bad business. Nikos Mechanikos doesn't like the idea either. He says we should build a concrete pool that will save me money.

"John, when you excavate in front of the house to create a level terrace you will need a retaining wall to stop the house slipping."

I agree.

"It will become one side of the pool," he adds. "A plastic pool is too light. My concrete pool would be like another great box to help hold up the house."

"Nikos, you have a good point; but a plastic one is guaranteed against earthquakes and other acts of god, whereas a concrete pool with tiles can crack and that's the end of the pool. Anyway, I must have everything finished by 9 September, when Peter arrives."

He takes this as a personal attack on his ability to get the work done. "I have already built six pools this year."

I stop the argument; rowing in front of the workers is bad for morale. The bosses must stand united.

Nikos Bulldozer has heard these arguments before and leaves. His philosophy is to do one job at a time and then plan the next one. "We must make a road, before we can make a pool." He wants to get going with his bulldozer. He will see us *avrio*, tomorrow.

Pavlos then leaves once he has realised that a good job on the road wall would be rewarded by the larger one in front of the house.

Nikos Mechanikos stays for lunch, a huge Greek salad and Jannie's chicken, asparagus and mayonnaise salad. He likes Danish food. His wife Anna is well, and the girls are growing fast. Our difference is forgotten for the moment.

"We'll all come for a swim in September?" he suggests with a grin.

Saturday 16 June, 3 down and 44 to go

The weekend should be relaxing, but Fred is coming today. Fred has performed miracles in clearing the jungle where the road is to be built.

At five to ten, I hear that familiar Canadian voice. "Hiya, John, how are *ya*, buddy?"

Now that summer has arrived, Fred has been sheared; all facial growth has gone leaving a cherubic face. I tell him so.

"Maybe forty years ago I was a cherub. What's on today?" he asks.

We go and inspect my great idea, which we have brought over from England. In the back of our old Land Rover Discovery are three enormous Swiss rolls. We take the top one out, unwind its length and then extend it sideways. There on the ground lies the solution to slipping mountains, a 6x3 metre mesh, rather like a huge aertex vest. I had seen them being installed along the bank of the channel tunnel rail link, to hold up the embankment. The manufacturer of the Erosaweb, who talked of "a cellular matrix of interconnecting polymer strips that form pockets to locate the fill material", guaranteed that any slope of 45 degrees would hold fast. As the land falls away at just this angle from the line of the road we shall build, I hope they are right.

I plan to lay the three panels just before the corner of the road to prevent the road slipping along the crucial point where the slope is steepest. Costing £350, it will be cheaper than a wall, which is liable to slipping anyway.

Fred and I go and inspect the proposed site for the Erosaweb. It is below the end of the previous wall, which slipped where an underground river had undermined its foundations. The evidence for this was growing even now, a group of innocent looking bamboos, always the tell-tale sign of water. Either side of this copse is an olive tree, surely strong enough to hold any minor landslide.

I leave Fred to cut away the almost tropical jungle. An hour later he calls up. "I'm ready, Big John, what's next?"

We stretch a panel over the stubs of the bamboo. This sounds easier than it is. On the flat, we have no problem in extending the matrix. Now on a 45 degree slope, with daggers sticking up to hinder progress and threaten our legs, we struggle but succeed.

"I need a beer," says Fred.

"But we have two more panels to lay," I protest.

"I'm a union man, I know my rights," he replies. "It's time for lunch."

Lunch for Fred is always a tin of sardines, a chunk of bread and a beer. The break gives him an excuse to have a moan. He has problems with some of his Greek neighbours. I ask him why he stays on the island.

"I like it," he sings back, he fancies himself as a bit of a folk-singer. Every so often he breaks into song, "Know that one, John?"

Fred isn't cheap. "You can get an Albanian if that's all you'll pay" is his standard quip. He tells the most disgusting jokes. But he's reliable. Give him any job and it will be done well.

The next two panels are pulled into place. Fred starts clearing the boundary. He leaves me to secure the Erosaweb by driving into the ground long steel pins along the edge of the panels. Soon I hear a cry for help; Fred has disappeared over the cliff into the jungle. He can't get out. I get a rope and he ties it round his waist. Now saved from falling further, he cuts bushes and brambles with his secateurs and passes them up to me. I praise him.

"Fred, I've decided I prefer you to an Albanian."

"Oh, you naughty boy," he replies.

Saturday evening is always our evening out. Costas, the new owner of *O Yiannis*, welcomes us. He has now been open two months.

"How's it going?" I ask.

"Very well; my mother is doing the cooking."

At his opening evening after Easter, which we attended as long term guests of his predecessor, he had asked my views on the cooking. Having just received a free meal, it was difficult to criticise. Referring to the *sofrito*, the garlic and veal stew, a Corfiot speciality, I said "the meat was tender, the gravy was thick, but where was the garlic?" He thought that tourists would prefer his version, but I was concerned that his target market must always be the Greeks, who keep him going in the long winter.

In Greece, there are three main types of cooking: the grill, the *meze* of many starters and the casserole or "pot" as we prefer to call it. *O Yiannis* is the best pot restaurant on the island and Costas is carrying on a long tradition. I am welcomed into the kitchen, standard procedure in Greece.

The lid of each pot is opened, a powerful aroma of herbs floats up and the contents are prodded to show that it is veal, lamb, pork, chicken or rabbit or fish, squid or octopus. Sometime he has snails and mussels. All have succulent sauces and many contain vegetables, such as little onions in *stifado* and mushrooms with chicken in white wine and saffron, Jannie's favourite. Then we move to the vegetables, *tsigarelli* which is spinach and hot pepper or paprika, giant beans in a thick tomato sauce, wonderful potatoes *fournou*, cooked slowly in the oven with lashings of olive oil, oregano and lemon. Finally, we look in the ovens, where the favourites of *moussaka* and *kleftiko* are sitting. I remember Jannie saying Costas's *taramasalata*, full of garlic, is the best she's tasted, even better than her own home-made recipe from smoked cod's roe as one can find only in a Danish smokery. I prefer the aubergine baked with feta, a dish called *imam* during the Turkish occupation. For Jannie, I order the chicken; for us I chose *sofrito*; and for me, the octopus and the *bourdetto*, the fish baked in a tomato and paprika gravy. Today, Costas has dog fish or *bakaliaros*, the salted cod. I prefer the former. Long gone are the days when grouper, the best of all fish, was on the menu.

Costas is delighted that we like the food so much. "What about the *sofrito*?" he asks.

"Tell your mother, it is perfect," says Jannie.

We now turn to business. I have to contact my neighbour, the previous owner of the restaurant. He goes and finds the telephone number of Yiannis Kremonis.

"But he may not want to see your plans," explains Costas. "He came round last week and had a few too many. On his way home on his scooter, a building came out and hit him."

Sunday 17 June, 4 down and 43 to go

I prepare a one minute speech in Greek about how my wall would come up to our common boundary and then ring

Yiannis Kremonis. He either doesn't understand or doesn't care. I feel I'm almost legal.

The rest of the morning is taken up driving another fifty steel pins into the bank to hold fast the Erosaweb. I notice Spiros spying me from top room of the Bellevedere Apartments, where he serves breakfast and an evening meal to his German guests. He always complains that they never drink enough, so bar takings are poor. I suspect that one of the reasons why they don't drink too much is that the descent from the bar to lower rooms, down dubious steps, is dangerous. From an English-speaking German guest, I learn that this is not mentioned in the travel brochure. One frail old man actually told me that he had chosen Spiros's as he liked the idea of staying by the beach: "only three minutes from the sea" according to the brochure. He'd obviously forgotten to bring his skate board to descend the mile to the beach!

I move up to the box on the boundary through which the road will be cut and, with a piece of string, measure out the turning circle of our Land Rover. I can then mark out, with the bamboo Fred cut, where the corner of the retaining wall will be. The drive-up will be very tight, particularly in the corner itself, where the road will be so narrow that the car can only just squeeze through. I repeat the exercise where we will build the new terrace, and find that, with a five point turn, we will be able to manoevre the car round in the area between the pool and the boundary. *Spiros is still looking.*

At the narrowest point of the new terrace, there is just enough room for the veranda and a pool with tiles around it; so I mark out their location. *Spiros is still watching.*

Finally, I mark out the new bedroom at the end of the terrace, making the house L-shaped, and the two new bathrooms, one en-suite to the new bedroom, the other en-suite to the original master bedroom. *Spiros is still looking.*

It is time to face my neighbour and have the first long conversation since the lawyers were involved. I go next door to make sure Spiros doesn't mind my plans.

"Good morning, Mr. Wallace," he says in his best English.

"I will make a road up," I tell him in extremely poor Greek, waving my arm to indicate the route. "It is not a problem, is it?"

"No, but you also make a pool?" he asks, in Greek this time.

Of course, he had guessed.

"Yes."

"How big is the pool?"

"Thirty-two square metres," I say.

"Mine is bigger, mine is fifty," he replies. He is now very happy. "How much will it cost?"

"Five million," I reply. Ten thousand pounds for a completed pool seems good to me.

"Very expensive, mine was five million and bigger than yours." His grin gets wider.

"But have you an electric pool cover?" I indicate, with more waving of arms: "On, cover opens. Off, cover closes."

"OK, Mr. Wallace, very good, pool not expensive."

We then get into discussions about leaves falling off trees and other things, which I don't fully understand. We part, honours shared.

I have checked with my neighbours so I can now tell the police that, when Nikos Bulldozer turns up, Councillor Mazis has given me the go ahead.

Having a pool sounds exciting, specially one whose surface is over the top of an olive grove yet appears to disappear into the sea way below. However, the dangers that arise are huge. We have been told numerous stories of small children drowning. So, first, we must build a wall between the veranda and the pool with safety gates to stop the little ones getting off the veranda. And, secondly, we must have railings to stop them falling off the terrace beside the pool.

I hope that, for much of the year, we can live outside, just as the Danes do through the long days of their summer. Eating, drinking and talking with friends and family on the veranda could become our principal activity. The big children could be playing in the pool and the little children could run riot along the length of what will become our outside living room.

Monday 18 June, 5 down and 42 to go

Today, another glorious one, will be a rest day, before Pavlos and Nikos Bulldozer start work. I phone Elena Manessis, who is free. We go into town, order three mini gates from Grammi and, picking up Elena, go out to her daughter's house, which is situated in the centre of the island. Away from tourists and traffic, it offers total peace, although on the way there we see the foundations for a new development being dug.

The Greeks are a cunning lot. Planning regulations demand four thousand square metres of land for a house off the main road. Building four small townhouses, which will easily sell to ex-pats retiring to the island, will bring in more money than a single house. To make them legal they call the houses 'apartments'.

Agalis and Rob, both artists and sculptors who live in England, have been building their dream house for five years. The villa is mainly single storey, with a vast living room and two bedrooms downstairs and the master suite above the kitchen. In front, looking south west to the mountains of the west coast in the distance is a veranda and a pergola. Either side, wings, one for guests and the other with studio and garage, enclose the secluded central area. The plan is exactly the same as Scandinavian farmhouses with their barns on either side forming the shape of a square with one side missing. Built of dark stone, it could win an architectural prize.

The only problem is that it is not finished. As is typical in Corfu, work is only carried out when the owners are on site.

This is a warning to us: we must complete the majority of the construction before we go home in six weeks time.

Tuesday 19 June, 6 down and 41 one to go

Pavlos's Tuesday has arrived. I wait. Nobody comes. I say hallo to Michael, our friend who owns the Romantic Palace on the beach and the Romantic View across the road below us. He gives me the Greek two cheek kiss. He finds it funny that I'm waiting. Finding a builder is one thing, he says; getting him to work is another. It seems builders are terrified of having no work, so agree to every proposal. It was now a case of who shouts loudest gets the builder to come.

I then discuss with Michael our need for new tiles. He says that he always uses Moskou in Agios Ioannis because their price is fair and their service is excellent. We decide this is good advice and go off to find them: around the Sinarades bypass, past the builders' dumps, Pelekas on the hill, down to the Ropa Valley and right at Parelion. Driving on the island is a great pleasure as long as one keeps away from town. Sasha, the happy 30-year-old receptionist, with brown eyes and brown curly locks, smiles at the mention of Michael. We look around and see drainpipes, bricks, windows, bags of this and bags of that.

"We've just moved here, so we haven't everything on display yet," she volunteers. She shows us a panel of terra-cotta coloured tiles.

"They don't break." She drops one; it doesn't.

"It won't scratch." She pulls a blade across the tile; no mark.

"Ideal around a pool; you can't slip." We believe her.

"They are Klinker." We have heard of Clinker bricks, baked at a high temperature, so we nod wisely.

"They are made in Greece, under licence from Germany." This means to me low cost and good quality.

"But not made in England?" I query.

She smiles and points to a drainpipe, made in England.

"And what about the price?" I ask.

"You will discuss it with Spiros." She points to the inner office where the boss is in a meeting.

"And what about the colour?"

"Ochre, Grey, Peach, Granite or Ceramic?" she offers.

It was all happening too quickly, but Jannie liked them. Seeing I was less impressed, she points to patterned strips with geometric designs in two colours. I'm sold; I could see the long veranda with a border half a metre in. Rhombus or oval? Either would be lovely.

It's now down to business, with Sasha as translator. Spiros offers a 15% discount to a friend of Michael; honour is upheld and a deal is done.

I ask about roof tiles. "I have 75 square metres of traditional tiles and I'll be adding another 65 for a veranda. I like beautiful old tiles; can you get more?"

"Yes, but other people are looking and there are not many around, so they'll cost you a lot," replies Spiros, quoting me a figure for 65 square metres.

"And how much will 140 square metres of new tiles cost?"

With the help of his calculator and the offer of the discount, Spiros comes up with a slightly higher figure.

"In which case, I will swap your new ones for my old ones," I suggest.

I've caught him out. We haggle a bit and agree on a low price, but with us holding our old tiles until buyers are found. So we will get a new roof, with new tiles, for almost nothing.

We go into town to check the cost of the same Klinker tiles at another tile shop. Michael was right; Moskou offers a very good price. It's good to have friends.

Nikos Mechanikos comes to check out my layout for the road and the pool. The plan is fine but we argue about the height of the pool. Nikos is stressed out. The council architect who was due back today is still on holiday, so we still have no permission.

"Let me tell you about a pool I designed in Lefkimmi," Nikos says. "The permission was a month late. I go down to tell my client so he could start work, but what do I find? He has completed the pool. I tell him that if the police had seen it, we would both be in prison. Next day, the police do turn up and ask for his permit. He tells them I have it in town, so they visit me. They look at the date and ask me how come it's taken the client only a day to build his pool. *It's a miracle*, I tell the police."

It seems the police are now after Nikos. So he doesn't want me to start work until we get the permit. The September completion date is looking hopeless; at this rate we won't even start by then. Nikos likes his lunch though. Sitting out under the shade of the huge olive tree, with the breeze cooling us, our worries are forgotten.

Wednesday 20 June, 7 down and 40 to go

Another glorious day comes, but Pavlos and Nikos Bulldozer don't. I go up to George at Texaco to ask his advice. Who should be there but Pavlos putting the roof on the water tank. I go into the office and find Nikos Bulldozer sipping his iced coffee.

"Nikos, can you start today?" I ask.

Nikos shrugs his shoulders.

"What are you doing then?" George asks Nikos.

"Nothing."

"Then go to John."

We drive on to Kastellani to buy bread, warm from the oven. The bakery runs the hardware and seed shop for the surrounding countryside, a sort of one-stop shop for builders and farmers. We buy a pickaxe-spade, the all purpose tool on the island. Shaped like an adze, it digs, scrapes and shovels.

We return home, overtaking Nikos, who is bringing his JCB down the main road. We walk up the old track. He points to the Erosaweb and I tell him it is to hold the land up.

Only the fact that his English is not too good stops him from telling me what he thinks, but I can guess. First he removes the bottom four of our sixty-six steps, so he can get on to the land. With my bamboos as a guide he starts, with surgical precision, to carve out the mountain as if it was cheddar cheese.

Down go the legs of the JCB, out goes the arm and he drags down some earth. Up come the legs, forward goes the JCB, climbing a little way up the path he has made and the process is repeated. Suddenly I hear a scraping noise. We investigate and find the top of the old soakaway which we had lost. It's huge and covered in a concrete slab. We remove its lid and look inside. Its walls, made of huge stones, look solid. With a bamboo, I test its depth. It is nearly three metres deep, with half a metre of mud at the bottom, above which is clear water. Nikos asks me why not keep it. I like the idea, but expect Pavlos to be disappointed.

Within an hour, Nikos has reached the top and comes down again smoothing all the way. I now have a perfect road. He goes up to the top again and digs out a trench with three steps: the base for the concrete box on the corner, where the wooden frame will sit. Down legs, scoop, turn, drop earth; scoop, turn, drop earth; up legs, move JCB down hill and repeat. A few minutes later I have a perfect corner.

I phone Nikos Mechanikos and tell him we are finished and the good news about the soakaway.

"Why don't we make another box just below the old slipped wall? We can now afford it. It will help hold up the road at the critical point," I suggest.

He agrees.

The two Nikos talk on the phone and digging starts again. We now have another, smaller, trench with a step in it. He's left a gap between the two trenches, so that if either box slips, it doesn't pull the other one with it. Nikos Bulldozer asks me if it's what I want. Throwing a large stone onto the slope, it happily rolls down to the main road below. I now have a perfect 25% roadway. He points to the Discovery.

"Try the road out", he says.

I put the car into first gear, low ratio and differential lock. We slowly ascend. It is fantastic.

Nikos initially refuses my offer of an iced coffee, but I have already made him one. He takes just one sip and quickly says that he needs to go.

I at last sit down under the olive tree and make the first of many schedules: Wednesday, 20 June, bulldoze road; Thursday 21, erect wooden frame for boxes; Friday 22 pour concrete; Monday 25 fill boxes with earth so we can bring the bulldozer over the old boxes; Tuesday 26, excavate in front of house; Wednesday 27 build frame for retaining wall; Thursday 28 pour concrete. We can start on the pool on 2 July. Construction is easy really.

I phone Nikos Mechanikos and tell him the work is finished. First he is very concerned about building without permission. Then he listens quietly to my schedule and then tells me my walls will fall down, as I haven't put any steel in the wooden frames before pouring the concrete.

"John, you must be careful. I understand that you have dug the holes, so you can put pressure on everyone. I'll get my steel man out to measure up on Monday."

Thursday 21 June, 8 down and 39 to go

Every day is a beautiful day, but today will be the best. Pavlos will come and build the frames. He doesn't appear, so I go up to see George, where I assume Pavlos is loading the wood. The wood is there but no Pavlos. George is also keen on getting the wood off his forecourt. He phones Pavlos, who explains that his nephew has been killed in a car crash. He has to go to a funeral tomorrow, so he will start the following Tuesday, one week after he originally promised. Having heard about the funeral the architect had gone to, I understand that this is obviously a standard Greek excuse. I am also surprised that he would be away five days. It's on the mainland, I'm told. I agree to a delay, only if we can pour concrete by Friday next week, so it can dry over the weekend. George passes on Pavlos's assurance - he will ready before then.

I phone Nikos Mechanikos with the news. He is doubly happy. First, there is a useful delay, so he won't be in trouble with the police. Secondly, the architects have met and say the building is "beautiful". I ask him to congratulate Anna, his wife, as she is the artistic one. I tell him he's the practical one; he's the one who will get the building completed.

We return to the Pavlos problem.

"Nikos, I think we could be in trouble. We've dug a great big pit in front of the old slipped wall. If we get any rain, it will slip into its own grave."

Nikos likes this wheeze as he knows that Greek builders don't like walls or buildings slipping into holes that have just been dug. He phones Pavlos who promises that his partner will do the work the next day and over the weekend, but Nikos must get the steel. They will deliver the wood that evening.

Sure enough, a truck turns up at 6 p.m., tries to back up my pristine earth road and digs itself in. The road is also too steep to slide the wood off. I suggest they return, go up the main road, round the hairpin bend to the top road and then drop the lorry load over the edge of the vast wall that overhangs the property down onto the shelf where the house is built. I try to ignore the remote chance that a beam or a plank would slip over the shelf and career down the hill, through the olive grove, and spear a tourist waiting at the bus stop on the lower road. Just in case, I hide in the house so that I won't get the blame. I hear a mighty roar as a ton of wood comes over the edge and wait for the screams from below. None comes; all the wood has stayed on the shelf. It looks as though Pavlos's nephew's funeral is only going to be a minor hiccup.

That evening we go down to have a meal on the beach at Theodoros. We order pan-fried fish, plus a half litre of their wonderful white wine. While Maria cooks and Jannie sips her drink, I swim. To the south is the bay, with the cliffs and the cave, sweeping out to Ortholithi, and with olive groves climbing the mountain to Pentati. To the east, is an empty beach; all the tourists have gone back to the hotel to eat or into the little resort to try out a new taverna. High above the bay, the mountains, still void of buildings, swing round to meet up with the road over from Sinarades, which comes down, past the hairpin bend, into which Spiros's Bellevedere and our Iliovasilema are squeezed, past Michael's Romantic View and the Pink Palace, back to the beach. To the north, the mountain goes out to Aerostato. A thousand feet below, huge boulders had fallen into the sea, now forming a deep natural swimming pool, never visited as it is two miles along the beach and too far for the tourists to walk. In the distance to the north, the mountains continue to fall, almost sheer into the sea, with the little monastery above Myrtiotissa, Laurence Durrell's 'most beautiful beach in the world', glinting in the evening sun. To the west, the golden globe falls slowly below the gentle sea, colouring the sky through reds of every hue. Jannie waves me in; it's time for eating and talking.

Tassos, the younger son, has watched our progress with both interest and amusement. "Now that you have the wood, the builders must come and do the work", he says.

"When?" I ask.

"When they need the wood for another wall."

Friday 22 June, 9 down and 38 to go

Morning comes again; we wait for Pavlos's partner to start on the frame but he doesn't come. It is time to check out the latest excuse with George Texaco, who will soon get fed up with me. Half the wood is still on his forecourt, so that's the reason for the delay. A few minutes later, Pavlos's partner turns up and starts loading up the rest of the wood. We go off to town and return to find an empty forecourt. We stop to pass the time of day with Caroline.

"Good news, the wood has gone," I tell her.

"Bad news, it didn't go in your direction", she replies.

I phone Nikos Mechanikos, who finds Pavlos is still on the island. He hasn't gone to the funeral yet.

"He's promised me that his partner will work over the weekend," says Nikos. "I have phoned my friend to come round on Monday to measure up for the steel. If the frame is not finished he will be very angry, as he trusts me."

Saturday 23 June, 10 down and 37 to go

Nobody comes. I decide to use my spare day siphoning the water out of the soakaway. An hour later we hear shouting from the road below. Councillor Papadatos has come to object. The water has wandered down the hill and reached his house. I hope I haven't made an enemy as the building work will be illegal once Pavlos arrives – if he ever does.

Thoroughly depressed by the evening, we go out to find friendship. It is time to check out the Crossroads Taverna. Vassilis and Eleni welcome us with open arms. They sit us outside. In the country, the night is dark; we are in the shadow of the hills up to Pelekas to the west; and Corfu Town is too far to the east for its lights to brighten the sky. Between the branches above, stars twinkle. Surprisingly little traffic passes: the tourists are in their all-inclusive hotels.

Vassilis brings us the menu; it is very short – a good sign that the food will be fresh as they promised.

"What do you recommend?" I ask.

"The rabbit *stifado* is excellent. I saw the rabbit, it was very plump."

"And is it fresh?"

"Last night I shot it myself," Vassilis explains. I look surprised. "Just down the road from here," he adds. Surprise turns to shock. "Only joking," he says.

"I don't like rabbit," states Jannie emphatically.

Rather than spoil her meal, I declined the offer and we moved on.

"As well as the grill, tonight we have *coq au vin*, *sofrito* and lamb in mushrooms," says Vassilis.

Predictably, Jannie chooses the chicken and I go for the lamb. In England, we are rightly proud of our Welsh lambs but, because of the cold climate, they always have fat on them. Their Greek cousins are pure lean meat. I am certain that if I ask Vassilis where it came from, he could, this time in all honesty, tell me from which field.

Sunday 24 June, 11 down and 36 to go

Our wall builder doesn't come. My first job is to mend the holes in my road made by Pavlos's lorry. I then spend the rest of the day moving the wood from what looks like a bonfire for Guy Fawkes Night, across the property, and stack it neatly above where, one day maybe, the new boxes will be built. I phone Nikos Mechanikos at home and tell him the bad news: he must put off his friend who will be coming out next morning to measure up for the steel. He remembers the details of the corner box and asks me the length of the new box hole.

As we sit glumly at home, I tear up my first schedule. Perhaps Nikos is right: you cannot have a plan in Greece.

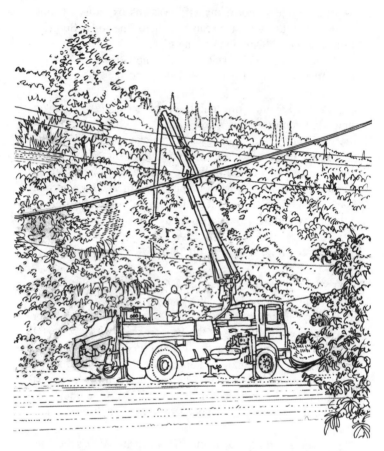

The pump is parked on the main road blocking the traffic. It raises its huge upper arm, straightening its elbow, until its forearm is high above the olive trees and the three electric cables stretching from Spiros's to a pole lower down the road. The operator moves the arm sideways and sees a problem: the slightest error will cause the arm to hit the cables and Agios Gordis will have lost electricity as well as water in the same day.

Creating a crisis

Monday 25 June, 12 down and 35 to go

A new week arrives, but Pavlos's partner doesn't. I telephone Nikos Mechanikos, who tells me how he had been right: you cannot have a programme. Nikos phones the steel man, who is furious as he'd put Monday by in his schedule to come out to Agios Gordis. He tells Nikos to find someone else.

Nikos phones me back and tells me the bad news, but he'll get another man. "Now we have the architects' approval, we can move on to Phase 2. I will get static approval on Thursday and early next week I will get mechanical and logical approval. This leaves the final phase, legal approval, once you get the papers from Parelion."

I don't understand all the technical jargon, but I am impressed; in fact I sense Nikos now has a plan.

"I have phoned Pavlos; he's still on the mainland but will be over tonight. He says that he will move the wood tomorrow and build the frame on Wednesday," says Nikos.

"He doesn't need to move the wood," I tell Nikos. "I've done that already."

"You've what?" he exclaims. "John, in Greece, the client must never do that; you will lose your dignity." I was more interested in getting the work done than my dignity. "Phone Pavlos tomorrow at nine o'clock and say to him '*perimeno*', 'I wait'."

Now my Greek is pretty lousy, but *perimeno* is one of the words I've learnt. The secret of getting the supplier or bureaucrat to get a move on is to say the magical word in reply to his excuse for inaction and then sit down and wait and

81

wait and wait until the boss, or person in authority, comes and agrees action.

Tuesday 26 June, 13 down and 34 to go

Another big day arrives and so does Pavlos with his partner and two workers. I offer them iced coffee. They refuse: Nikos Bulldozer has probably warned all the workers of my dreadful English coffee. They inspect the hole for the corner wall. Then Pavlos sees the trench for the second box.

"Megalo problima," he says.

He carries on telling me why it is such a big problem, but my Greek doesn't extend that far. I want to tell him that his problem is not a big problem – it's only four metres long – and it is not really a problem at all but a solution. It will stop the land slipping down into the main road below.

Up until now, all my retaining walls have been built by others. Now I could see it done in front of my eyes. I was the engineer (and coffee maker). Pavlos gets his partner to hold vertically a post at the downhill corner of the trench. This is held in place by a plank nailed to a nearby olive tree, forming a supporting strut or flying buttress. Another post at the corner of the future road is attached to another olive tree. The wall of the original box, to which we will connect our road, acts as the third vertical post. Horizontal posts are nailed to the vertical posts, and then vertical planks are nailed to the horizontal posts. We now have the outside frame. They repeat the exercise with the land wall of the box. The wood for the corner box is finished, all within three hours. It is now time to move to the smaller box. Pavlos shrugs his shoulders and mentions *ksilo*, 'wood', and *avrio*. I ask him to phone Nikos, but he doesn't want to then. He promises to do so in the evening. I report back to Nikos and warn him about the small box, the wood, the tomorrow and the phone call which, of course, Pavlos never makes.

Wednesday 27 June, 14 down and 33 to go

Avrio arrives. It is now two weeks since we arrived in Corfu. We wait for Pavlos. I then phone him and say *perimeno*. He talks of noon and a truck; he is obviously going to get more wood and finish the job this evening. I report back to Nikos and check again about the steel man. Yes, he has found a man. He has given him the measurements and the steel will be delivered *avrio* or *methavrio*, the day after tomorrow, Friday. This sounds good, particularly as Nikos assures me that if they put the steel in on Friday morning, Pavlos can "close" the frame on Friday afternoon, by building the inner wooden wall. Maybe we can pour concrete on Saturday.

Every hour I phone Pavlos. First it's "a few minutes", then it's "an hour", then at two o'clock he says the words which haunt me: *"ehi halasi"*, "it's broken". He is probably referring to the lorry. I panic, phone Nikos and ask him to phone Pavlos. He refuses as doing so would be a loss of dignity. Maybe our problem is not lack of planning but loss of dignity.

Thursday 28 June, 15 down and 32 to go

I walk down the hill to Spiros 'Mini market' Mazis to get bread. It's crystal cool in the morning after a clear night. Ahead is the mountain of Garouna, rising five hundred metres from the valley, covered in olive groves almost to the top, where vineyards grow *kakotrigis* below cliffs at the summit. The view is pure Alpine.

"We had a meeting last night; we passed your plans," Spiros says. "The papers should be prepared today or tomorrow."

Returning home, Jannie tells me she has found a snake in the gutter. Elena says kill it. Maybe it is only a slowworm, but the Greeks kill everything.

We wait for Pavlos who will build the wooden walls for the small box. At ten, a large lorry arrives, not with wood, but steel. Panic, it can't be for us, Nikos said Thursday or Friday. I phone Nikos, yes, it's for us. Jannie, who is watching the drama, calls up from below that the lorry has gone down to the valley. I give a sigh of relief – we want wood today, not steel. A few minutes later, Jannie calls up that the lorry must have gone down to turn round as it's here again. Nikos, still on the phone, boasts that his people are always on time, but where is my man, Pavlos? He'd never work with men like that.

I phone Pavlos. "Where are you, Pavlos?"

"I am on the road to Agios Gordis," he replies.

By now, the lorry is unloading the steel, three steel men assisting. At that point Pavlos arrives. There's a minor traffic jam and lots of shouting. The youngest of the steel men comes up and starts gabbling away. At that moment I wish I could speak Greek properly. I hear the word *café*.

"Hot or cold," I ask.

"Three iced coffees, please." The steel men are happy. The wood men, meanwhile, have backed up further than last time - my road repairs have worked. They start to drop off more wood.

What do we do? I phone Nikos whom I can visualise, head in hand, thinking: one lorry, one truck, two teams and six men.

"John, we are in trouble, the police will come. They will ask for your permit and we haven't one yet." He then suggests both teams can work together.

I doubt the wisdom of this, but go down to tell Pavlos that he should start on the second box, while the steel is put in the first and that, if he has any questions, he should talk to Nikos, now. But Pavlos has disappeared.

I phone Nikos again.

"Good," he says. "Why be in trouble now with the police, when next week we will have the permit? If the police come,

Pavlos will blame me and say that the engineer phones him every day. Let's wait. If they do come, tell them that you have permission and the permit is in town. Also say that everything is very dangerous, the old walls will fall down. Therefore we need the new walls."

Obviously, two lies make a truth.

In the meanwhile, the steel men are building a cage inside the wooden frame. They place bricks at metre intervals along the bottom of the huge trenches and then lay long thick steel rods on top. More rods are put at right angles and they tie each intersection tightly with wire. We now have a mesh. A second mesh is then created above the first and the two are held apart but locked together by attaching steel supports shaped in the form of three sides of a square.

With the base of the cage in place they add vertical 'L' shaped rods to the mesh to form the uprights of the walls. These stick out above the wooden frame as perhaps one day I will need to raise the height of the concrete. Finally, they hold the uprights in place by attaching long horizontal rods. Wherever two rods cross they turn wire to form a tie. The cut, turn, twist, tighten action is performed at an incredible pace. In five hours everything is finished and the steel men leave.

My siesta is broken by a nightmare of walls falling into holes. I decide we really must go in to town and see Nikos so we can plan the next visit of the steel men. Spiros Zervos, Petros Kardakis's original partner, is holding court. Nikos and Anna are there in a good mood, discussing the plans which the architects have approved. They talk about 'pride'.

"I hope not 'pride before a fall'," I interject, referring to the future building.

"No, John," says Spiros, explaining everything with the one sentence, "remember, we are from the Orient."

By that I understand him to mean how important it is not to lose face.

We discuss railings with Anna, the aesthete. She likes our choice - simple with little curls between the uprights. "They match the oval pattern of the tiles," she says.

"Traditional," I add, not to be left out of this cultural exchange, which usually goes straight over my head.

Nikos, meanwhile, agrees that, if Pavlos completes the frames the next day, we should try to get the rest of the steel put in on Monday.

"If he doesn't, we'll throw his wood in the road," he suggests. He pauses and adds, "Maybe not, we need him."

"Why?" I ask, now fed up with delay.

"Because he's been building without the permit and will blame me."

Friday 29 June, 16 down and 31 to go

I wake early and hope that, with the steel in place, Pavlos will be able to close the corner box and build the outer frame of the lower box. Pavlos arrives at 9.00 with his team of three and they unload yet more wood. He directs work from on top of the old boxes.

"You'll close the corner now?" I ask.

"Yes," Pavlos replies.

I point to the lower trench. "You'll build that today?"

"*Einai ena problima.*" He replies. There is always a problem. I ask him to speak to Nikos Mechanikos.

I go to the phone; Nikos is not in the office. I phone Anna. He may be on his mobile, she says. I try his mobile, Anna picks it up. He's left it at home. I'm on my own now.

Pavlos comes up to the house. I ask what the problem is.

"*Ti einai to problima?*"

"*Thelo solines.*" Pavlos wants pipes.

Why would a wall builder need pipes? To let water through the wall, of course. I offer him some empty plastic water bottles. Pavlos is not impressed.

I make a rapid exodus to Kastellani, to our bakery and hardware store. At the ridge over the mountain I see a recently constructed wall, get out, and measure the diameter of the pipes and the distance apart. I work out that I need 20 pipes each 30 centimetres long. I search the yard for 6 metres of pipe, go in and pay. I buy a saw as well, as I am sure Pavlos hasn't one. I feel like a real builder.

Rushing back, I find Pavlos has disappeared. I phone Nikos, who is now in his office.

"Please phone Pavlos; you can also find out if he'll finish today," I plead.

"No. I'm doing my tax today."

To make him feel guilty, I tell him I've got the pipes.

"Oh yes, we need pipes," he tells me.

"Please phone Pavlos," I ask him again.

No, he won't but he'll speak to the man left in charge. I look up 'boss' in the Greek dictionary, *Efendiko*. I like that, a good Turkish word, *Efendi*.

"*Efendiko!*"

He likes to be called this and willingly comes to the phone. There is much heated discussion. Why are Greek conversations so heated? Nikos comes back on and tells me that Efendiko had promised to start on the little box today and finish it *avrio* or *methavrio* (I had understood this bit) and we could put the steel in on Monday. Hold your nerve, John, I say to myself; have a cup of tea; wonderful.

At 11.00, Pavlos turns up and by 11.15 they've stopped for lunch. The first side of the corner has its inner wooden frame in place. They start again at 11.30. At least Greeks work hard once you've got them. The trouble is getting them. At 12.00, Efendiko comes up again.

"*Lathi.*"

I look puzzled. Oil, olive oil? He shows me a jack like thing. I find him some WD40 and get a big grin from Efendiko, who obviously sees me as a friend. I investigate and find metal rods have been inserted through the two walls, with clamps outside and inside the frame. The jack turns out to be a tightening tool; wall building is a bigger job than I thought.

At 12.15, the banging noise stops. They've gone, I think, but I soon hear the noise of a pickaxe. They are starting on the lower box. Nikos Bulldozer has dug the trench at the wrong angle. An old man with grey hair appears over the boxes wall, my wood pile starts to go down. Planks are handed down to workers below and hammering continues at a frantic pace.

"Can life get better?" I ask myself.

Maybe they will finish the outside frame of the little box this afternoon. I watch as the wood rises up. Effendiko, who speaks a little English, explains that he has a problem. There is no way the frame will be the two metres wide I had measured for the steel.

"They will be 1.60 metre." He cannot make the box any wider as he needs space outside to tighten up the frame.

I phone Nikos to tell him the good news; he can get the steel for Monday; and the bad news, that the rods will be too long. I tell him I am a "Waller, not a Wallbuilder". He doesn't understand my joke but promises to be out in two hours. My prayers have been answered.

Nikos phones: "I've a problem, I can't come now, but I'll come over early next week."

"But that's too late, the steel won't fit," I plead.

He laughs when he understands my concern. "We can always bend the steel."

Saturday 30 June, 17 down and 30 to go

To keep up our spirits, we have promised ourselves that every Saturday we will eat out. In the 70s and 80s, we had no option but to go into Corfu Town. Now we can visit the many restaurants on the beach. They have, over the years, moved up-market from 'something and chips'. Many offer excellent

Greek cuisine at prices little more than the tavernas where the locals go. Any excess charge seems only fair as their season barely lasts six months.

But tonight we are looking for something special. We want the traditional Corfu atmosphere plus the best music we can find but it must be near at hand. So at ten we make for a new taverna on the road between Sinarades and Pelekas – *Platopigado*, 'the square of the well'. It is run in the perfect Greek manner. The mother cooks, the son and daughter serve and the father makes music. Only Greek is spoken.

The lamb, for which everyone is waiting, slowly turns on the great spit. For those who cannot wait any longer, a kilo of small lamb chops are provided on a large plate which is put in the centre of their table. Hands reach for the top of the pile and the succulent meat is ripped from the bone to the great satisfaction of the carnivores. The friend of the family, who is in charge of the grill, is getting hotter as he labours in front of the charcoal. He stops for a beer. Flames appear, he steps back and all the meat catches fire. He has another beer and the fire dies down. Nobody seems to worry. Meanwhile, plates of Eleni's exotic starters are brought to our table by Yiannis, a delightful young man with a pigtail.

By half past ten, we inquire whether there will be music. Angelis, who was the director of the village philharmonic, shrugs his shoulders. His fellow musician has not arrived, so maybe we'll have music or maybe we won't. At last a small man carrying a bouzouki turns up. At eleven o'clock, the music starts, the lamb is served and the party begins. Angelis is a virtuoso on the keyboard and sings beautifully. A second half-litre of his *Petrokorintho* wine appears, courtesy of the house and accompanied by a gorgeous smile from young Alexandra. Our duo is joined by a tall tenor, who knows he has the looks as well as the voice. The crowded room joins in as song follows song. Someone gets up to dance: it's a personal matter. Later a fine lady comes on to the concrete floor and seductively moves to the music – her partner kneels on one knee encouraging her. By one in the morning, everyone is joining in, arms stretched out linking dancer with dancer. It is time for us to go. We are happy again.

Monday 2 July, 19 down and 28 to go

Monday is always a good day. After a weekend working on the property, I can spend a week watching others work. By 9.30, our enthusiasm is lagging: the steel men haven't come. We decide to let things happen; phone calls are pointless; we must get the permit. The drive to Parelion raises our spirits. Would our paper be ready for us? I look for Sophia, who is not expected until 10.00, so I go up the stairs to find the English-speaking Spiros.

"Sophia hasn't prepared your paper," he says. "No problem, I will."

There and then, he goes to a PC and copies from the minutes the date and place of the meeting, the page of attendants and then the single paragraph resolution saying that the commune had no objection to my plans. Ten minutes later, I come out waving my piece of paper. I tell Jannie that Greece is a remarkable place: action is either *tora* or *avrio*, now or never.

Waiting in the car, Jannie had been watching six men directing traffic anti-clockwise round their new invention: a circle painted on the road, their new roundabout. As only one car goes by each minute, we question its need. Each driver approaches the junction, slows down on seeing the obstacle ahead and decides to go to the left, to the right or straight over. The angry officials, showing off their authority, start shouting and indicating that the circle is a roundabout. They leap out of the way, swearing and cursing, as the confused driver nearly runs them over.

We go on into town to give the paper to Nikos, who is at the *polodomia*, what we guess is the planning office. His days are always the same: the mornings waiting for the bureaucracy to move the paperwork, the evenings on his PC, creating more paperwork. Visiting sites only happens early in the morning, before the bureaucrats are awake, or in the afternoon, when they are having their siesta.

Our next stop is at our accountant, who is changing the ownership of the property from the company we had to set up back in 1971, to ourselves. Amalia is her happy self.

"We are nearly there," she says.

I have always been wary of this expression; most of my life, programmers have been telling me this. But when it's accompanied by a huge smile I melt; and we leave a contented couple and return home to meet the steel men. The steel men haven't come.

Tuesday 3 June, 20 down and 27 to go

Nearly three weeks into the project and we still haven't poured any concrete. Anyway the steel men will definitely come today. I pass the early hours, before the sun comes over the mountain and the heat builds up, cutting bamboo into three metre lengths, future markers for the building above. At 9.30, I phone Nikos to tell him that the steel men have not arrived. He suggests I phone him again at 10.00 if they still haven't arrived. They don't come, so I phone.

"Don't worry, I have just talked to the boss, they are bringing extra steel."

Back to the bamboo; the saw breaks. I fix it by hammering in a screw where the metal pin has broken off. A few minutes later the blade snaps, so we go to Kastellani to get a new saw, costing all of 600 drachmas (£1). The owner of the hardware store decides that we can save the saw and put a new blade in it. This will save me some of my 600 drachmas. He screws, wrenches and hammers away. His assistant then has a go. Finally another customer tries. The screw is at last removed, the blade is inserted and a bent nail is driven in. Here is another example of the Greek fix-it philosophy. They benefit to: having paid for the blade, I splash out on another saw.

On our return, there are still no steel men. Nikos promises they'll definitely come *avrio*. We agree to meet Nikos Bulldozer and Pavlos at three for a council of war. This becomes four o'clock but Pavlos has decided he won't come until the steel is fixed. At 4.30 Nikos Mechanikos arrives, inspects the boxes and issues a few English swear words.

"The small box is too small for the steel we've ordered."

I don't tell him that is exactly what I said on Friday. We decide that we won't have the uphill wall of the box, so now we will have just an ordinary wall. I phone Pavlos, who by now is probably asleep. He gets his wife to be the intermediary. He won't come, but he will see Nikos in town. Nikos comes to the phone and, after a few Greek swear words, he tells Pavlos to come and remove the bottom planks of the uphill wall, so the steel can fit. He agrees to come next morning before the steelmen arrive. As a contingency, I learn which planks to knock out.

Meanwhile Nikos Bulldozer has arrived with his friend, Nikos Merianos, who we are told is the best builder in Sinarades. I immediately take to him and, with so many Nikoses already, christen him Nikos Builder. He is barrel-chested, slightly balding, and has a huge smile. He tells us that, like most Greeks, he has spent time at sea and has visited Liverpool, which he obviously liked as the others have a good laugh when he tells a story about England and its women. He turns to me and, with a disgusting grin, says in passable English.

"I'm looking for English wife."

I promise to see what I can do; he probably thinks this could be the bonus for a job well done.

He looks at the roof and offers to replace it with brand new tiles as they are easier to lay and they'll look like the old ones after a few years. I explain that I have already ordered new ones for the veranda and the extension; but I would prefer the old ones as I like the traditional look. He agrees and tells me to cancel the order as he'll find enough old ones from the village. I fear that there could be a lot of roofless houses in Sinarades this winter.

They then discuss the extension. Nikos Builder wants to dig the foundation by hand; Nikos Bulldozer prefers his machine. Nikos Mechanikos supports the high tech solution, but turns to me, the client.

"John, what do you think?"

"All I want is a schedule on when we can build the road up so we can get the bulldozer over the old boxes," I reply sulkily. "Can we pour the concrete by the weekend and can Nikos Bulldozer fill in the corner on Monday?"

We then plan six days in advance. Is this a record? I note that Nikos Builder has joined the 'no plan' team as he doesn't have much faith in Pavlos. Nikos Bulldozer just wants to get the job done as soon as possible, while Nikos Mechanikos despairs of everything that he is not controlling. I can't suggest that maybe that was the answer: he should take control. At the beginning he had agreed to be my engineer as long as I did the site management.

I reckon that next Tuesday we could excavate the bank in front of the house and on Wednesday Pavlos could start building the retaining wall in front of the house. Nikos Bulldozer then says he needs an extra day to dig the foundations of the extension. I am now convinced that we should dig them by hand. The two Sinarades Nikoses leave with my possible new builder saying: "No problem, I can do *ola*, everything."

Seeing that I am depressed, Nikos Mechanikos says. "You think things are bad now. In a week they'll be alright. Remember, in Greece, construction is like Zorba's dance. It starts slowly and then speeds up."

At that moment, Nikos Builder returns.

"If Pavlos doesn't come when the steel is in, I'll do it and I'll also pour the concrete."

Suddenly this new Nikos has become our favourite, our Action Man.

We walk down to Theodoros on the beach. A twenty-minute stroll is followed by a swim, then a meal. Building worries disappear. Fotis, the elder brother, confirms that Nikos is a good builder. We discuss the problems of Greek workers and the Olympics.

"I think there's a 90% chance the Olympics will be finished on time," says Fotis, "and the work will be good."

"At the rate I'm going, there's a 90% chance I will NOT finish on time," I suggest.

"You must realise that the Greeks only work if there is a crisis."

"Then instead of time management, it will be crisis management," I promise.

Wednesday 4 July, 21 down and 26 to go

Next morning I wake early. "How can I create a crisis?" I ask myself. Yesterday they had promised that by next week I would have a flat terrace in front of the house, on which the pool would stand, and just in time for the date that I had booked for the pool to arrive. Piscines Ideales had asked me to confirm I was ready, the week before. Instead of postponing its arrival, I decide to let the pool come.

The one detail that still has to be worked out is how one gets from the new terrace to the house. Everyone agrees that the twelve steps along the short side of the pool to the veranda would make something like a *bodzo*, the traditional Corfiot construction of a balconied first and main floor which is accessed by stone steps. But what would we do about wheelchair access? I have a brain wave; we will make a ramp beside the long side of the pool, furthest from the house. Louise will like this as the children will have less far to fall if they climb out of the pool on the seaward side. Peter will like this as Des can get Sean's pushchair all the way up. The workers will like it as they can wheel their barrows up to the higher level. And maybe one day, I will like it when I get my four-wheel-drive zimmer frame.

At that moment I hear shouting. Michael, of the Romantic View below, is screaming at Spiros to come out from Bellevedere Apartments next door. I call down to see if I can help. As Spiros is twice Michael's weight, Michael might need some assistance. Nikos, Spiros's son, appears; obviously Spiros is scared of Michael in this mood. It turns out that Michael's hotel reception is full of mud, water and shit. And it's Spiros's shit. The one way conversation consists mainly of the word *Malaka* – wanker. Nikos promises that the sewage lorry is on its way, which doesn't placate Michael as the damage is done. We smell its arrival and go out to watch the fun. They remove the cover of the tank, which increases the smell, and Michael again comes out to join battle.

At that moment the steel men come in their 4x4, with the extra metal hanging on the back. Chaos is complete. The steel men have their priorities right. "*Frappé*," they say.

Two iced coffees coming up. I'm not sure if it's a compliment to the cook or a concern for their health. The shit wagon soon moves off, Michael goes and we get down to work. They look at the sketch of the new box. Since it was originally planned it has almost halved in width. They point this out. I had forgotten, with all the excitement of the sewage, that Pavlos was meant to be here to take off the bottom planks. But he isn't. Therefore the contingency plan must go ahead. I borrow an all-purpose walling tool; I thwack and within a few moments we have a three-wall box. They seem to think this is the most normal thing in the world to do.

The two layers of steel mesh are quickly erected. I phone Nikos with the good news, all is finished. I then move on to the bad news, my crisis. "Nikos, I forgot to tell you that the pool will arrive a week today."

"You can't take delivery; we haven't received planning permission," he shouts.

"But I have confirmed its arrival," I reply. There is silence at the other end of the phone. "But if we put in the pool first, then you can build the surrounds in one concrete pour," I explain. "It'll save time and money."

Nikos grunts agreement. I sense my crisis is working.

Now I have to motivate Pavlos. I doubt if the pool's arrival will interest him, but Nikos Builder's participation might. So I phone Pavlos. Mobile off. Could George Texaco help? So we drive up to the garage and who is there but Pavlos preparing the forecourt. I ask George's advice.

He calls over to Pavlos. "What are you doing tomorrow?" Pavlos makes some complicated reply. "No, you are not; you are closing John's walls and pouring his concrete."

"George, I owe you one," I say.

"Make it an English lunch," he replies.

"No, make it a Danish lunch," says Caroline.

I ask him if he knows Nikos Builder.

"Yes, he's my cousin."

"Is he a good builder?" I ask.

"The best in the area; he built our house."

"Then why didn't you mention him when I asked who could build my veranda and extension."

"Because he is so good, everyone wants him and I knew you were in a hurry," he answers.

I have been warned. I phone Nikos Builder to get him to give me a quote for the veranda, roof and extension. No answer.

Life in Corfu is more than work – there is sleep. The siesta is a great invention for the knackered and I am really knackered. I doze off and, what feels like seconds later, I am woken by what sounds like the war: loud bangs and cracks of rifle fire. I go out to investigate and see Michael below.

"4 July, American Independence Day," he explains, "why do they start now when we are all asleep?"

Dr. George, at the Pink Palace, is married to an American and his guests are mainly from the States. It is obvious that for this day of the year, they will take over. Until late at night, disco music blares out and fireworks go off continuously. But there is work to do. I cut more bamboo and make more phone calls. Alexos Hirdaris, Piscines Ideales' man in Corfu, is expecting my call. He says that he will check that Athens is ready for next Wednesday and then he will come out and meet Nikos Bulldozer next Monday at 6.30. The crisis develops.

Thursday 5 July, 22 down and 25 to go

Another lovely day. We should pour concrete this afternoon. A new crisis arises. Poor Michael below, after being shat on yesterday, has lost his water. He's in the road below shouting at Spiros Alamanos, the district plumber, whose job is to keep the water flowing. Water is gushing out of the mains onto the road, just before it reaches Michael's pipe. A few minutes later, Michael's neighbour, P.C. Poulis, joins the discussion. They are then joined by Councillor Papadatos, who also has no water. Spiros Alamanos gets his axe and, with a single mighty stroke, knocks off the concrete covering the pipe where the leak is. More water pours out of what seems to be an old join between the two very old and rusty mains pipes that lie along the road. He tells the angry crowd that he'll turn off the supply and then fix the leak. He gets into his car and drives off.

By now the first of Pavlos's workers has arrived. He was inspecting the waterfall, while drinking his iced coffee. The rest soon turn up and within two hours the box's inner wooden wall is finished and locked in place ready for the concrete to be poured. Pavlos phones the concrete company which says it can't get here before 3.00, so he announces that he'll pour tomorrow. I phone George Texaco telling him the problem and how the pool arrives next week.

"Put Pavlos on," George says. "I'll tell him that, if he doesn't pour today, we'll get someone else."

Pavlos's team is in uproar. They had thought they could have an early day, but now they will have to work in the afternoon. They agree to be back at 5.00.

Alexos, our pool man, phones. I'm impressed. I'm the one who normally does the phoning. He wants to talk to Nikos Bulldozer. He needs some rocks under the pool; they'll act as ballast to hold the structure from slipping off the mountain. At 5.00, I hear the noise of a great monster below. The elephant has arrived, the machine with the great trunk which pumps out the concrete. Pavlos is sitting in the shade of Michael's Hamburger Van. This eyesore, probably brought from Germany when Michael and Anna started business in Corfu, usually sits there neglected. Now it has a use, a protector from the evening sun.

The pump is parked on the main road blocking the traffic. I ask Spiros next door and Michael below to get their guests to move their parked cars. The great machine is ready for action; its four legs are extended and then lowered to stop it falling over. It raises its huge upper arm, straightening its elbow, until its forearm is high above the olive trees and the three electric cables stretching from Spiros's to a pole lower down the road. It now slowly bends its wrist so its long hand turns downward over the cables. From its hand, it drops the long hose, which looks like an elephant's trunk, right over the corner box. It is ready to pour the concrete. The operator moves the arm sideways and sees a problem: the slightest error will cause the arm to hit the cables and Agios Gordis will have lost electricity as well as water in the same day. He gets on his mobile phone; the conversation is very heated. They'll get an even bigger pump, but not today. He drives off.

Five minutes later the first ready mix concrete lorry arrives, soon followed by a second. "Where's the pump?" asks the driver, still eating his ice-cream.

"It's gone," says Pavlos.

Pavlos, probably more afraid of George Texaco than me, gets on his mobile. He's trying to get a bigger pump from the other concrete companies. But none can come out this late. To calm me down, Pavlos promises me that the boss of the pump company will come out tomorrow.

"And pour the concrete?" I ask.

Pavlos shrugs his shoulders. I don't say that it is a pity that the boss hadn't come out to look before he sent his pump. By now all of Pavlos's team has arrived. They hear the news, lots of M-words. I tell Efendiko to tell Pavlos that the pool arrives from Athens on Tuesday, so we must pour tomorrow, Friday. Pavlos again shrugs his shoulders: that's my problem, it's my crisis.

I phone Nikos Mechanikos. No answer. I leave a message for him to phone me back.

Nikos phones back. I think he's secretly pleased; the site manager is making a cock-up. "You should have warned Pavlos about the cables," he suggests. "I'm sure they have a bigger pump."

"Is there any news from the *polodomia*?" I enquire about the planning office.

"I had it in my program for today, but a friend of mine has had a car crash, so I didn't go. I will tomorrow."

We set off for town. A good things about Greece is one can do a second day's work in the evening – everybody is open. In fact, it seems that construction goes on in the day and planning goes on in the evening. We pop into George Texaco on the way to tell him the news.

"You should have built the road in March," he volunteers.

He's right, of course, but the threat of a fine for not having a permit was my excuse. I think most Greeks get on with the work and then arrange that they have no bother if the police come round before the permit is issued. That's difficult for a foreigner.

As we drive in to town we discuss George's comments. Maybe what was happening to us was usual in Corfu. In which case, it has been sensible to go for the pre-fabricated pool. The thought of making more wooden frames, pouring more concrete, and then having to tile the pool was too horrid to contemplate. Let's hope we don't have the same problems with Piscines Ideales. We visit Grammi, who provided all the doors and windows for the house and who have an order for the three gates off the veranda. I have measured up the future pool terrace, and so we place an order for a railing for the edge of the terrace. The last thing we want is our latest grandson to run off and over into the olive groves below. Grammi promises that the railings will arrive in August.

Friday 6 July, 23 down and 24 to go

Today is the last day for pouring the concrete if Nikos Bulldozer is to fill up the corner boxes with earth on Monday. I finish laying the remains of the Erosaweb and then wire all of it up to the steel in the frames. I wait for the bigger pump, but it doesn't come, so I phone Nikos Mechanikos at 11.00 to find out what is happening. Spiros Zervos tells me Nikos is at the *polodomia* finalising my permit.

"He'll be back in the office in half an hour and will let you know."

It turns out that Pavlos has told Nikos that the Proskyr pump is too small, which Nikos already knew, and that he has booked a bigger one from Markezines, the other concrete supplier. He will phone Nikos as soon as he knows when it will come. At 2.00, I phone Nikos who is on his mobile. He will phone me back. At 2.30, the bad news breaks. Markezines can't come with the pump, and the boss hasn't been out to look, which I know. Pavlos tells Nikos that maybe he can get a big pump out on Monday.

Faced with the plastic pool, which he doesn't like, coming on Wednesday, concrete taking three days to dry and the permit which we still haven't got, I am happy that Nikos is still trying to solve our problem. He suggests that maybe we could pour concrete from the main road above. Jannie and I measure the distance to the corner, 38 metres. We phone Nikos back. It's too far; the arm and the hose can only go 30 metres.

He then suggests that we widen our earth road at the bottom by cutting away the old steps up to the house, so we can get the original pump up the road, where it can work well away from the overhead cables. At that moment, we hear a noise from below. It's the pump? No, it's Spiros's shit wagon, what a stink. And to think Nikos Bulldozer will be working over Spiros's septic tank which is half on my land. What a terrible accident could happen if he went through its roof. The trouble is the courts might not think it was an accident. All of us on the whole mountain are fed up with Spiros and his shit. Once the season is over, his septic tank is never emptied. I have been told that over the winter a trail of sewage can be traced from the valley up to Spiros, even by a blind person. Fotis and Tassos have at one point recommended dynamite, but I think they just enjoy the fight between their friend John and his enemy. Michael on the other hand has a vested interest in demolishing the tank.

I phone Nikos Bulldozer, whose English suddenly gets worse, so matching my few words of Greek. "I do not understand. Please tell George Texaco your plans."

I think he senses a trap. George, already up for a second lunch at this rate, phones Nikos Bulldozer, who says he can excavate on Sunday. Nikos Mechanikos, pleased with progress, promises to phone Pavlos, whom he will get to come on Monday to pour the concrete. Just in case, I phone Nikos Builder as I am beginning to lose all confidence in Pavlos.

Saturday 7 July, 24 down and 23 to go

Saturday in the West is usually a day of rest, but in Corfu building goes on. I phone Nikos Mechanikos to make sure he has contacted Pavlos.

"How are you, my friend?" says Nikos.

"I've been up early moving the wood, so the pump can get up the road," I reply. "Pavlos won't have any excuses."

I suggest we go over to Proskyr to make sure the pump is here early Monday and check its size.

"Don't worry, John, Nikos Bulldozer knows its size and anyway all the concrete companies are closed today. All you need is that the pump can get under the cables." At this point, his voice becomes sad. "The problem has been that I didn't take responsibility - for the builders, the steel and the pump. I should have seen the problem of the cables. I never have this problem with my workers."

He pauses and then realises that I may take this as a slight on my efforts. "John, if you could speak Greek, I know you could have made everything happen. You are the best worker."

We agree that, on Monday, Nikos Builder, who knows what we are trying to do, should meet our pool man Alexos Hirdaris.

"He's the blond one, isn't he?" asks Nikos.

"No, he's the dark one, who wears dark glasses and looks like the Mafia," I reply. "He's young, even younger than you." He takes this as a compliment, which it is.

I go off down to the valley to get a newspaper. I meet Councillor Papadatos, P.C. Poulis and Spiros Alamanos inspecting the water main. Where Spiros demolished the concrete cover only two days ago, there is now a fountain. To make the repair he had cut out 30 cm of rusty pipe and replaced it with the same length of shining new pipe. The pressure was too great and now we have a buckled mess of metal. I follow the water, a happy stream, all the way down

102

the road to the valley, pick up a paper and return to find a permanent solution has been found. The down-stream rusting pipe has been raised by a brick and the up-stream pipe has been tied to Michael's rarely working supply pipe – Greek ingenuity at its best.

Moments later Pavlos arrives. "Where is my wood?" he asks, in Greek.

"*Eki pera*," I reply, there beyond. I had learnt this in my Greek lesson thirty years before. I complete the ditty, "*pas eki tora*", you are going there now. This delights Pavlos and we continue in Greek.

"Good, Nikos Bulldozer is coming tomorrow," says Pavlos.

"And when is the pump coming?" I ask.

"Early on Monday, maybe at noon."

"And when will the concrete be dry?"

"On Tuesday, so Nikos can fill up the boxes with earth and finish the road," replies Pavlos.

"And when will you start at the top?" I ask.

"Thursday or Friday."

I turn to Pavlos's partner. "What is your name?"

"George," he replies, "George Segal."

"And I'm Paul Newman," says Pavlos.

I laugh. "And I'm John Kennedy."

I thought to myself. "Nikos, my friend, this is management – in Greek."

Without a care in the world, Jannie and I set off for a day out with some visitors to the island. We're tourists again. Our friends have been staying on the west coast, so we take them to the northeast coast. The little harbour in Nissaki is crowded with boats and holidaymakers. We return home and realise that our lovely beach of Agios Gordis is relatively empty, because it is so long.

After the last load of earth has been dumped and shoved up into the corner and around the bend by Lefteris, they are ready to go. Nikos's JCB is already upstairs and is joined by the Caterpillar. Our three champions pose for a picture between the two yellow monsters, with Ortholithi in the background.

Building the road

Monday 9 July, 26 down and 21 to go

Early morning comes with a taste of summer. Ortholithi has disappeared into a sea mist. The sun will burn it off soon and we'll have a scorcher. At 8.00, I phone Nikos Bulldozer. His mobile is off. I phone his home and his wife answers sleepily.

"Is Nikos there?" I ask.

"Yes, one minute."

Nikos is on the phone.

"Are you coming?"

"Yes, now."

I feel today is my personal Olympics. If we pour the concrete, the Greeks will finish theirs on time. Soon after, Nikos arrives and starts his assault on the steps and the wall. The JCB Sitemaster Plus is in good hands. The small scoop pulls and digs, the big scoop shoves and carries.

"Where do you want the old concrete steps?" Nikos asks.

"Up the road, they act like boxes," I reply.

The big scoop opens its mouth, grabs four steps in its teeth, perhaps a cubic metre of concrete, and disgorges it just below where the lower box will be built. The small concrete blocks are dropped on the bank of the earth road, totter and settle. How they fail to roll down into the main road, only Nikos knows. He's a true professional. He shoves earth on them in order to widen the road so that the pump can fit. Then he does a three point turn and, digging in the big scoop which is now downhill to maintain balance, starts to move the little grab erotically from side to side, smoothing the road he has made. Other grown men want to run a railway for a day, but

105

I'd be just happy with a JCB. I'm brought back to earth as he then starts demolishing the retaining wall beside the steps and on top of Spiros's septic tank. It's the critical moment.

"What are you doing?" shouts Spiros, who has been watching from his bridge.

Unseen, he has arrived with his son Nikos as both linguistic and physical support. They would be a good match for Nikos Bulldozer and me.

"The pump can't pour concrete from the main road below, so I'm widening my road to get it on my property," I reply.

"Why not pour the concrete from the top road?"

"It's over forty metres," I claim knowingly.

By now the grab is attacking the retaining wall of the steps. The lower part is just poured concrete and is not reinforced by steel rods from the side wall of the septic tank. I breathe a sigh of relief. The upper part of the steps' wall contains rods from the retaining wall above the back of the septic tank, which holds up steep land either side of the once disputed boundary fence. The grab tears bits off, leaving eight twisted rods sticking out, like the tentacles of some hideous buried octopus.

Spiros shouts at Nikos Bulldozer that if the back retaining wall is demolished, the land will slip and Bellevedere Apartments will collapse. I smile at the thought of his building falling into a pit of shit. Nikos is not amused; he swings the grab at Spiros, who recognises his match and retreats. I reassure Spiros that I will be extending the retaining wall by ten metres.

Nikos finishes. The bulldozer driver is the king of the construction industry. I must buy his daughter a Danny the Digger book. Within an hour he has demolished the lower steps and their retaining wall, carried them up the hill to the boxes and widened the road so the pump can work.

"Nikos, you are the best," I said, "Would you like a coffee?"

"Yes, why not?"

"This has been a good day. Pavlos will be here at twelve and the concrete will be poured this afternoon."

"That's not possible" replies Nikos. "This morning I phoned the concrete company, Proskyr. Pavlos has not ordered the concrete."

In panic, I phone Nikos Mechanikos who calls Pavlos, who claims that he ordered the concrete from Markezines, the other concrete company, and we will have it by 12.00. End of panic.

Nikos Bulldozer is rewarded with iced coffee, English style and inferior to the Greek version. We discuss my three problems: I leave for England in three weeks, the pool arrives from Athens tomorrow evening and I haven't got his money. I tell him that he will be paid tomorrow and that Pavlos will only be paid when he's finished the work. Nikos rather alarmingly suggests that Pavlos shouldn't be paid until next year, obviously the standard method in Greece. As he leaves I remind him that we will see him this evening when we all meet to discuss with the pool man what has to be done.

By 2.30 there is still no Pavlos. I phone him.

"Problem, problem, problem!" he explains, and finishes with: "No concrete."

Nikos Mechanikos phones him. "Pavlos now says that Markezines cannot deliver today nor tomorrow."

Nikos then phones Proskyr to see if Pavlos can get the concrete from them tomorrow. They are slightly surprised.

"But Pavlos is getting 50 cubic metres for another job."

So the truth is out. Pavlos was finishing the other job, so we have been lied to. Nikos threatens him again and Pavlos agrees to come after finishing his other job. I trust people too easily. Nikos calms me down; Proskyr have never let him down.

At 5.00, who turns up but Vassilis Proskyr himself in his huge Toyota 4x4 truck? He checks that he can get the pump up our wider road. I then take him up to where we will build the retaining wall, the veranda, the terrace surrounding the pool and the foundations for the extension, all to be finished in two months. He says he'll have no problem – in fact I think he likes the project. There is a lot of concrete to pour. In hindsight, I wonder why he didn't come last week. Perhaps it was because I hadn't made a proper plan. As Proskyr is leaving, he asks about the house.

"When was the house built?"

"Thirty years ago," I tell him.

He's surprised, perhaps because of our current lack of management. "Who was the engineer?"

"Petros Kardakis."

Vassilis smiles and says. "He is the very best."

Jannie and I sit down for a quick cup of English tea and discuss Pavlos. Should we get him to do the surrounds of the pool or ask Nikos Builder to help us out? I think Pavlos should do it, but we shouldn't pay him until he has finished everything and that we should tell him we were going at the end of the month. Jannie wants Nikos Builder; she thinks that if I have anything more to do with Pavlos I will have a heart attack. To get some advice, we decide to go and see George Texaco.

His car wash is due to arrive in two days time and he still hasn't finished the preparatory work. I tell him about Pavlos and the latest cock-up.

"But he's laying concrete for me tomorrow," he says.

So we now know who his mysterious client is. George still reckons we should stay with Pavlos and pay him on completion.

At 6.30, Jannie disturbs me from my bamboo cutting.

"He's here."

I hope that it isn't Alexos Hirdaris as I need Nikos Mechanikos to explain why we are not ready for the pool. But it is our pool man. I am in for an awkward thirty minutes.

"I'm sorry I'm early," says Alexos. "I'm taking my grandmother to Kato Garouna," referring to the village to the south up the mountain.

"Wouldn't she like to go up now? It must be very hot sitting in the car," I suggest.

He isn't worried. "Tell me about your Trojan Horse," he asks, pointing to the wooden frames creeping up the mountain. "How will you pour the concrete?"

I tell him how the pump came last week and how Nikos Bulldozer has widened the road so it can come back tomorrow. It seems an excellent excuse for the delay.

"But you have to do that," he says. "You are not allowed to pour concrete from the main road in the tourist season."

That is news to me. I have a vision of the police turning up.

"Excuse me sir, can I see your permit for blocking the road?"

"I'm sorry officer, I haven't got one."

"If you don't mind me asking, can I see your permit for building that wall?"

"Oh, well, I haven't got one of those either."

We move on to the subject of the bamboo poles which show where the pool will be. Those lying on the ground mark the plan and those stuck in the steep slope indicate the elevation of the pool. I reckon the top of the pool will be forty centimetres lower than the level of the floor of the house. Alexos disagrees; the pool will be level with the house. I lie down on the floor and tell him the horizon, out to sea, is above my cross marker. For fifteen minutes, we look at the bamboo poles from every angle. I find this a fruitful exercise as time is going by and he has still not mentioned the imminent arrival from Athens of the pool.

I finally take up courage. "Did you know that I ordered the pool for tomorrow?" I ask.

"Oh yes, I cancelled your order. Constantine in Athens always waits for me to call."

My crisis is over; it seems that I am not the only crazy client. At 7.00, Nikos Mechanikos arrives to discuss what Alexos wants.

"A retaining wall in front of the house and a wall around the peripheral of the pool terrace," he says.

"It's like a doughnut, with a rectangular hole in the middle being the pool," I volunteer. "Will the doughnut be solid?"

"No, the pool terrace will have a concrete roof connecting the pool to the peripheral walls with a void underneath," Alexos explains.

"And why do you want the outside walls built first?" I ask.

"Because building the retaining wall after the pool is in place could damage the pool."

The two other Nikoses appear. Nikos Builder is happy just to listen. Nikos Bulldozer, who wants to be told by Alexos what he needs, is easily satisfied. He will compress the terrace once he has carved it out of the bank. This I would pay for. The Athenians will then mark out where he excavates the deep end and pay him direct. But before that happens, we will make a retaining wall. He goes off to continue late into the evening on another site. His time management is most unGreek.

Alexos leaves to take his grandmother, probably overcooked by now in his car, up to Kato Garouna. We are now down to three. Nikos Mechanikos, in an aside to me, says that, for the next phase, he thinks that we should use Nikos Builder and get rid of Pavlos. I tell him what George Texaco had said and he has used them both. I also don't like putting all my money on one horse. If Pavlos builds the retaining walls and the pool terrace, Nikos Builder could, in parallel, re-roof the house and build the veranda and then the extra bedroom and two bathrooms. If Pavlos plays up again then we could always fall back on Nikos Builder. We agree. There will be no more argument for today.

The two Nikoses get down to technical discussions. I produce a schedule of work, which takes them both by surprise. They start costing each item.

"When can you let me know how much for the whole job?" I ask.

He thinks a moment and answers, "Now – £15,000." I am slightly nonplussed. He then adds the knockout blow. "I'll let you have this in writing tomorrow." I don't agree the price or he'll think he is charging me too little.

Perhaps Nikos's forecast last Tuesday, that all would be alright in a week, looks more likely now. Will tomorrow be the turning point in our project?

Tuesday 10 July, 27 down and 20 to go

As pouring concrete won't start until the afternoon and we believe Nikos Mechanikos when he said Proskyr had never let him down, we will spend this morning sorting out some paperwork with Nikos. Last night we agreed to meet outside his office at 9.30, so we pass the Texaco Garage at 9.00. Pavlos and his team are there, and seconds later the first concrete lorry turns up. The day has started well for George. We hope ours will go as well later on.

Once in town, we photocopy our passports and the original land ownership documents. We wait outside and see our engineer's moped parked opposite. Nikos Mechanikos appears, happy.

"Get your car and follow me".

As he zigzags in the traffic, we have no idea where we are going or even why, but eventually we stop and find a parking place in a taxi rank down by the port. Jannie is left to placate irate cabbies and Nikos leads me into a modern building seething with humanity. There are queues everywhere, even queues to get into the room where one queued.

"It's the day everyone comes to pay money, so you can come back tomorrow," says Nikos.

He points to some counters in a large room upstairs.

"That's where you will start." So we left.

Having spent an hour last night arguing where the top of the pool would come, we must now find the point in space, or rather on my bamboo, where the bottom will be. We will then have to excavate the sloping terrace and level it off to this point. We should have enough earth from the top of the slope to fill in the bottom of the slope. If Alexos is right, he can then place the plastic walls on the level land once Nikos Bulldozer has dug out the deep end. If I am right, the new flattened terrace would be 40cm below the mark on the bamboo. We will then have to either bring in lorry loads of earth to raise the terrace, or lower the pool, two steps down from the house.

We pick up a pencil-thin pipe from Profi and go back to the house to survey the land. We fill the pipe up so that it contains no bubbles, then check that the level of the water at both ends is the same. Lift one hand, the level goes down and at the other end it rises. Same level again, brilliant. Jannie holds the end at the house, while I mark the same level on the bamboo. It seems the pipe method confirms the 'look at horizon' method and that Alexos's spirit level eyes were wrong. I mark out three further points on the bamboo. If Nikos can bring the level of the land up to the highest, we'll need no steps; otherwise the pool will be one or two steps down from the house.

At one o'clock, we drive up to George Texaco to see how the concrete pourers are getting on – a hive of activity and no place for an impatient client. By 3.00, I am getting concerned and phone the concrete company Proskyr.

"No, don't worry, you'll definitely get the concrete today" says Yiannis at Proskyr.

An hour later, Nikos Mechanikos phones up. "Proskyr has just phoned me, they are worried; Pavlos has only poured 30 cubic metres out of the 50 he ordered at Texaco. At this rate, he won't finish tonight. Please go up and check what's happening."

This time, I venture into the garage. George reckons it'll take another half an hour. George Segal confirms half an hour and Pavlos, calf-deep in a paddy field of concrete, ignores me.

At 4.45 it is time for another visit. I find Pavlos's team in the shade drinking iced coffee. This time Pavlos is all smiles.

"OK, John, we are coming."

As if to confirm this promise, a ready-mix concrete lorry trundles passed - *it's mine*.

Ten minutes later the pump arrives at the house and launches itself up the now widened track which I boast is 'my road'. It halts just before falling into the old soakaway. Its driver and conductor, yet another Nikos, gets out of the cab and adjusts the pump's legs. There is no problem with the front left leg. The front right leg, however, needs some railway sleepers to stand on as it's on the edge of the bank falling down to the main road. Nikos the Pump slowly jacks the machine up and repeats the exercise with the rear legs. For the uninitiated, a pump is a cross between a giraffe, an elephant and a whale. Its three ten-metre necks slowly extend to let its trunk drop free. At the other end its whale-like cavernous mouth is ready to receive tons of food poured from the waiting ready-mix concrete lorry. This is the theory anyway. Unfortunately an eight metre high olive tree stands above the pump, so the neck has to battle its way through the branches.

Pavlos grabs the trunk and directs it at the lower box, pouring concrete into its base until the steel bars disappear. He is followed by George Segal and his mate with the 'cappuccino machine', a hose connected to an air pump, which blows concrete into the corners of the mould, and fills parts where other means cannot reach. The air creates froth and turns the surface from lumpy into smooth. The three move up to the bigger box on the corner while Nikos the Pump moves the neck and the flow of concrete with his remote control.

The plan is to fill the base first as this will harden before the walls are filled. Operations stop as we reach the farthest point of the future hairpin bend. The neck is now fully extended but we are still two metres short. Pavlos and his team pick up posts and planks, shout at each other, hammer away and soon have a platform level with the top of the wall. They all grab the trunk and together shove it until it is above the furthest corner. Heavy concrete rushes through in long bursts. They stand precariously on the platform struggling with the trunk and pour. George Segal directs the trunk and Pavlos drives a post deep in to make sure the concrete slips down to the base. Finally, Pavlos smoothes the top, making it a constant slope down the hill. With the wall finished, they return to the top and empty the third and last lorry load into the base. We've used twenty-one cubic metres - one more than my calculation and one less than the figure I gave Proskyr, including contingency.

It's time to put the pump to bed. The neck concertinas back. Nikos the Pump, who is delighted with the monster's performance, rewards it with a soft orange ball slightly smaller than a football. The animal is also delighted and sucks it up its trunk and "thwack"! the ball travels back to its stomach, clearing concrete from its throat. Its stomach is now a churning mass of concrete, which it releases, rudely, onto my road. Pavlos gets a shovel and shoves and pulls the turd to flatten it out. Lo and behold, from an earth track, I now have the start of a concrete road. The pump raises its legs and off home it goes.

It is now 9.30 and the sun has gone down. When Pavlos and his team did eventually come, they worked flat out. Maybe the Olympics will be held on time. As Pavlos is leaving, he turns to me and rubs thumb and index finger together, the international code for money. I tell him I'll talk to Nikos Mechanikos, which I do.

To celebrate, I shave for the first time in a week and we go for a twilight swim in the sea before going up to Georgy Porgy's for a victory dinner. It's taken four weeks to make our first wall, but we have one and it sure feels good.

Wednesday 11 July, 28 down and 19 to go

7.00 in the morning is a perfect time to inspect a new wall. There I am admiring the great building project when a happy Pavlos turns up. Nikos told me that I owe him, for 21 cubic metres at 13,000 drachma each, about £525 - good value. Pavlos is even happier when I say I have the cash. He asks if it is in dollars. Then his team arrives and strips the wood away from the concrete of the upper box; she's a beauty. When the break comes for his mid-morning meal, I call Pavlos up to give him his money. I had spent the morning preparing my speech in Greek, which I had written down. He reads it quicker than I could say it. This proves that my written Greek is at least better than my spoken Greek.

We now need Nikos Bulldozer to fill the road on Friday and excavate in front of the house on Saturday. No answer from his mobile. This is worrying as he, of all people, always has his mobile on. I phone his wife who says he's in the neighbourhood. She gabbles away with further explanations but it is all rather lost on me. He has to be out of mobile reception, to the west of the mountains. George Texaco says he hasn't passed, so we rule out Agios Gordis. We make our way round the bypass to see if he's in the country. On the road to Pelekas I ask an old man, tending his vines.

"Do you know where Nikos Bulldozer is?"

"Deutsch?" he asks.

His German is worse than my Greek, so he uses sign language to point up to the village, then makes a circular sign with his hand and points his index finger downwards. Confused, we drive towards Sinarades and come across a drum in the middle of the road, the local version of a mini-roundabout. We see a group of workers.

"Nikos Bulldozer?" I ask.

They point over the edge of the road. Far below is Nikos with his bulldozer, in a storm drain, loading up with building material. The alleyways are so narrow in the village that

Nikos uses the river and the drains to get around. Yes, he can make Friday or Saturday.

Then it's off to town to visit the mysterious office. Today there is only one other person there so, being British, I make my own queue. Behind the counter people are sitting around chatting and drinking coffee. I can see why being a bureaucrat is pleasant. It's now my turn. The delightful blond clerk asks me to fill in a lengthy form. It's all rather hilarious as the questions, about my father and about Jannie and her father and so on, are in Greek. She seems happy with my answers, or perhaps she's just a happy person. She points me to another office, where a man takes my form and fills in a register, then gives me a piece of paper with a number on it. I go back to my blonde friend. She takes the form, the copies of the passports and the deeds and a note from Nikos Mechanikos and starts entering the details into her computer. Occasionally she asks me to read a name, which she types in Greek. (To those that speak less Greek than me, I can only say what a fantastic language it is: it is totally phonetic.) She now prints out a few pieces of paper and then copies some of the details onto a cardboard schedule. Off I go again, to another office. There I find a man, who I assume is the boss, sitting at a large desk which is piled with files, smoking a cigarette and drinking his coffee while he ponders what to do next. He signs the documents that the computer has printed out and gives me another note. By now I have collected eleven pieces of paper. My smiling friend welcomes me back and works out that I owe £14, which I must pay downstairs. The cashier produces my receipt with three copies, two of which he keeps and one goes to my friend. I can now go.

All this, without a single queue, has taken just half an hour. No wonder Nikos Mechanikos had said that this process would take a whole morning on a busy day – so much for Greek bureaucracy, the bane of commercial life. But what have I got? I deduce the cardboard schedule is a log of payments and then the penny drops. I am now registered as an employer of sundry workers and it will be at the IKA office that I will be paying the Greek equivalent of their national insurance.

We take the schedule and the papers to Nikos's office and then call him to say we are ready to plan the next stage in the construction. A brilliant day suddenly turns ugly. Nikos, who is obviously rushed off his feet, joins us for a lemonade. I ask him if he will meet Nikos Bulldozer and Pavlos and explain what they must do. He again insists we shouldn't go with the prefabricated pool from Athens but make one in concrete. It is the same old row.

He draws his walls on one piece of paper and mine on another. "Look, you are duplicating all my walls," he argues.

"But your pool walls will be thicker than my walls and will cost more," I respond.

"And how will you support the pool terrace? I'll be making it at the same time as the pool," he continues.

I admit that I don't know the answer but I'll phone Alexos and let him know.

"My man can do it in half the time and you will save money," he says.

"But your man is not free or else I would have used him instead of Pavlos," I counter.

"But I could make him free," he suggests, sounding like a typical Greek builder.

"And you would manage him?"

"Yes," he promises.

"From Thessaloniki, when you are in holiday for two weeks in August?" I stand up. "With my Athenian pool men, I have guarantees," I add.

"And if they don't meet those guarantees, are you going to court?"

It has all got out of hand. I tell Nikos that we would have no more discussion.

"Normally, John, that would mean that you are on your own. But as you are a friend of Petros, I won't let you down."

Thursday 12 July, 29 down and 18 to go

Another beautiful morning. My lovely wall looks fine. As a contingency, I phone Alexos to check that he could manage the pool project, when we were back in England, if Nikos failed to deliver. He sees no problems as he won't be on holiday. We turn to the current problems and I tell him that the road wall is finished and we will have a road by the weekend with the retaining wall and the peripheral walls built next week. Therefore could he bring in the prefabricated pieces from Athens and erect the pool in the week after next? Again no problem.

We then turn to the pool terrace. "How will we support the terrace?" I ask.

"The steel rods that reinforce the plastic pool walls extend a metre up. These are turned to the horizontal and connected to the rods from the retaining wall and the peripheral walls," he answers.

It all sounded so easy. "And then you can come and fix the liner and install the equipment in the first week in September before my son arrives?" I ask.

"Yes, but I would like you to tile around the pool before we put in the liner."

By now, Elena is waiting in town. We pick her up and return back again to the centre of the island. She is very depressed as nobody has come to work on Rob and Agalis's house. This time, however, a couple of workers are there, and a little work has been done. Perhaps they knew she was coming. They plead ignorance when cross-examined on progress. I feel a little bit smug as I tell her about our wall. Elena, who spends much of her time in her garden, asks me if I'm doing any watering. She laughs when I tell her we haven't planted any flowers.

"Not flowers, but walls – you need to water the wall," she says.

Now, Elena knows more about concrete walls than most men. Her husband, George, concreted the mountain above Benitses to build the San Stephano Hotel.

That night I give the wall a really good soaking – I hope it likes it. I then phone Nikos Bulldozer to check that he is coming tomorrow. He says he's sorry, but he is finishing the work in the village. No excuses, just a straight answer. He finishes one job before going on to the next. This increases my respect for him. Yes, he will work the weekend and hope to finish on Sunday. I think of incentives, but feel this will cheapen what will be his best effort anyway.

Friday 13 July, 30 down and 17 to go

An early morning call comes from Nikos Mechanikos, a peace signal perhaps. "Have you watered the wall?" he asks.

"Of course," I reply truthfully as I had just giving it a second bath.

"It helps the concrete dry slowly and makes it strong," he explains. "Give it a good shower twice a day."

"It's my pleasure. Can we have a meeting with all the players in this great drama, early tomorrow?" I ask. "But we will only talk about my *plastic* pool, which is coming from Athens on Monday week?"

"OK," he agrees.

I phone Proskyr to find out where I could pay them. It seems a good idea to keep them on my side as it is obvious they know all about Pavlos's movements. My call is obviously a surprise as instant payment is not part of the Greek culture. Yiannis, speaking in very passable English, explains that they are off the Ropa Valley. The office is where they make the concrete. We make for the Ropa Valley, past our friends in the council offices. Cautiously, we check there are no other drivers in sight when we pass the new roundabout, where kerbstones have been added to the painted circle. The sign to Proskyr sends us up into the hills to the right, onto a lunar landscape where enormous bulldozers and lorries wander. We stop outside what looks like an office and Yiannis comes out.

"Mr. Waller? Coffee?"

Nice people to do business with. I give them a wad of drachma notes.

"17,000 per cubic metre and 50,000 for the pump," he says, "that's 400,000."

Like all Greeks, he folds the wad in half so each note wants to uncoil. He flips through them in a flash.

For £800, I have had four great hours of entertainment.

Saturday 14 July, 31 down and 16 to go

I get up at 7.00 to give the wall a final watering as today we will fill it up and make our road. By 8.00, I am ready for the gathering of the clan: the workers who, within the next eight weeks, must provide me with a pool, a veranda, a new roof and possibly an extension for Peter to stay in. The diminutive figure of Pavlos appears from beneath the wall.

"Where is Nikos?"

The first Nikos, Mechanikos, arrives a few minutes later and the two inspect the masterpiece. Nikos points to the steel rods sticking out of the inside of the wall and says that some will cause problems to the bulldozer later in the day. Pavlos goes off to fix them. It dawns on me why so many Greek walls look in need of a shave: their steel hairs have never been cut off.

At 8.15, I hear a tremendous clanging and banging. A Caterpillar bulldozer, with its huge tracks, appears. Who's this, I think, not recognising the driver? Then a gigantic lorry arrives, full of hardcore. At that moment our other two Nikoses turn up.

Nikos Mechanikos is soon in full flow, with the two other Nikoses listening carefully. There's only one boss, so I sit under the olive tree and listen. It is agreed to make some short cuts to save time. The original plan was to build thirty metres of wall, fifteen to hold up the veranda to the east of the pool, nine for the terrace to the north of the pool and six south of the pool, where the steps up to the house would be. The ramp down the west and seaward side of the pool was to be deferred until the terrace was covered. They now decide that the southern wall can't be built until Nikos Bulldozer's JCB has dug the deep end.

At this point, Nikos Mechanikos comes up with a brilliant shortcut. "We will make the frame for the retaining wall with only the outer side wood. The inner will be the excavated land."

Having agreed to complete the bigger project in a week, Pavlos now claims he cannot finish the reduced work by Friday. Remembering the farce over the steel, I suggest that if he orders the steel, for which I am certain he could benefit financially; I will then have only one backside to kick. The others like the idea as I haven't mentioned the words "metaphorically speaking" – I don't know them in Greek.

So finally we come to Nikos Builder as by now Nikos Bulldozer, the Action Man not the Talking Man, has left the meeting in order to direct the road building. "I'll build the extension for £14,000. You pay for the windows, doors, water heater and fittings," he says. His price had come down £1,000 since his first quote.

"Too much," I reply.

"OK, I'll pay for the water heater and the fittings."

"And what about the replacement roof and the veranda roof, 120 sq. metres in all? I told you Michael's man has quoted only £7 per sq. metre for laying the roof tiles."

"I'll charge £18, but this will include all the materials, lining, insulation and tiles. I will also replace all the rotten beams in the house and rebuild the wooden ceiling," offers Nikos.

I hesitate.

"And you'll only have one backside to kick," he adds with a delicious grin.

Nikos Mechanikos nods in agreement, so we shake on the deal. For £17,000, I was getting a bedroom, two bathrooms, a veranda and a new roof. I leave the two Nikoses to work out the payment schedule. I suddenly remember what is missing.

"And how much will it cost to have a fitted cupboard in the new bedroom, like the one in our bedroom?"

"£1,600," Nikos replies.

I could now see the catch. I would get a good price up front and then pay big costs for extras.

"And when can you start?"

"As soon as Pavlos builds the walls."

"Nikos, we are getting so much concrete; it will look hideous. Can we face some of the walls with stone?" I ask.

"Of course, but you must buy it yourself," he replies.

Is all this too good to be true? Meanwhile, the Caterpillar has flattened one load of hardcore. The soakaway has disappeared, but Nikos Bulldozer says he has put some concrete over the top and we can still use it. If we can find it, I think.

Nikos Mechanikos is off, a good day's work done. He has been at his best, totally in charge.

Fred has just arrived to add to the excitement. His first job is to create our first flowerbed, next to the old steps, into which we can transfer the geraniums from the olive tree terrace where Spiros had long ago made a jardinière. He carries up four big bags of compost. He's in his element. Well away from the war zone, he breaks up the clay and digs in what he guarantees will be just what the plants like. I think he likes plants more than people.

The second load of aggregate has been dumped and the road moves up the hill. There is a narrow entrance between the new retaining wall and the old slipped wall. Through this, the Caterpillar can shovel earth. Occasionally, a chunk of the old wall chips off, but my precious new wall stands untouched.

Fred, with his bed planted and watered, is ready for more action. We have to cut the top three metres off a five metre olive tree so that the pump can get the concrete up to the house at the end of the week. There is a lull in activity as they wait for the next load of hardcore. The road is now deserted. Now is the time to show the Greeks how a true Canadian lumberjack can drop a tree in the restricted space between the JCB and the Caterpillar. Fred cuts a wedge off the underneath, then a slice into the top, while I hang on to the rope for dear life. At the critical moment, I call "Help" and Fred dashes over. With a final pull, the top of the tree drops down within inches of the bulldozers. I feel pride in the Commonwealth.

The two stalwart roadbuilders come over and start stripping bits off the JCB, which has some mechanical problem, hammering them and putting them back. It is crude but effective. The monster springs to life. Fred and I are up against impending disaster – we have blocked the road. Fred, with chainsaw waving frantically, and I, tugging the branches and boughs up the steps, clear the road seconds before the next load of aggregate is dumped off. We retreat in victory to enjoy our tins of sardines and bread.

By now, the road has reached the corner. It is Nikos Bulldozer's turn to show his skill. He backs up the JCB with the pneumatic drill attached, ready for an assault on the most southerly of the original boxes, where he plans to hack a hole to get access to the terrace above. I watch as Nikos uses a crablike motion to manoeuvre the JCB sideways, then forwards and sideways again. Slowly but surely he turns the ninety degrees to face the boxes' wall. If he can get round the hairpin bend in a JCB, I can get round in the Discovery.

All seems to be going well, so Jannie and I go off to see Moskou to explain how we no longer need the roof tiles. This doesn't worry Sasha. Perhaps it is because everyone ignores my orders until the materials are needed. I then enquire about the glorious cream stone from Sinies in the northeast of the island.

"Have you any *siniotiki petra*?"

"No, but I have some beautiful pink stone from Albania," Sasha replies. I hesitate. She then adds her knock-out blow: "And it's cheaper."

"But I want the best, and that comes from Corfu."

I feel a little like Justinian when he rebuilt St. Sophia in Constantinople, insisting on the most beautiful stone and marble from throughout the Byzantine Empire.

"In which case you will have to go to the quarry in the mountains and buy some," she answers.

We go back home to a silent site. Everyone has gone. If this had been Pavlos I would be worried, but I have faith in Nikos Bulldozer. A few minutes later, he turns up with his tool box. The previous repair has obviously not worked. He gets to work and soon he is ready. In front of him is the small box on the boundary, with 50cm thick reinforced concrete walls. He has to hack nearly a metre off the top.

The deafening staccato throbbing of the drill is followed by the grunting of the bulldozer and the creaking of the concrete as a few centimetres of wall are prized off. Slowly the gap in the box grows deeper. Each block of concrete falls into the void below where, only this morning, I had been watering the base of the new wall. At long last Nikos has chewed enough concrete off and retreats making his way round the corner. He changes JCBs to his old faithful with the scoop at one end and the small digger at the other. Up the hill he goes, round the corner like a crab, riding his outer wheels like a wall of death rider. With the gap ahead of him, he extends the digger's arm and starts pulling earth down from the terrace above. Slowly the level of the road rises towards the bottom of the gap. Then, with a great roar, the JCB clambers over the old wall. He has won the battle; he has climbed the mountain and can now excavate and then flatten the sloping terrace for the pool.

He starts digging more of the terrace away, scooping it back onto my road below. Meanwhile the Caterpillar is shoving a third load of hardcore into the corner. The lorry driver comes up and sits on the old boxes and admires the beauty of the JCB and the Caterpillar dancing a maniacal two step, scoops and claws waving with passion.

They stop for a break and I meet the Caterpillar man, Lefteris, called after the Greek word for freedom. He is Nikos's partner. Built like a mule, he's a happy man, except he's not married. We discuss the chances of my finding him an English girl, but I have to tell him my daughter is married with three children. He doesn't come from Sinarades but Vouniatades, a small village over the mountains to the south. I ask him if he knows Stavros, our favourite waiter, who works at Taverna Pontis and also comes from the same village. He does. The truck driver now joins us. Marinos is also from Vouniatades.

"Yes, I know Pontis," says Marinos. "I'll be there tonight."

I decide that as Saturday is always our evening out, we will also go to Pontis. I am certain that Marinos, who speaks a few words of English, will be with a large party, a recipe for fun.

After the last load of earth has been dumped and shoved up into the corner and around the bend by Lefteris, they are ready to go. Nikos's JCB is already upstairs and is joined by the Caterpillar. Our three champions pose for a picture between the two yellow monsters, with Ortholithi in the background. Finally Nikos goes down my wonderful road and brings the JCB with the pneumatic drill up the hill. They leave and I wish them a good evening and say that we'll meet again next morning at 9.30.

I take a late siesta, then Jannie and I walk down to the beach and Theodoros for a swim until the sun goes down. As we sip our wine, we tell Fotis and Tassos of the great mountain road. I think they are impressed. What a way to end a working day, but the fun is still to come.

Spiritually refreshed, we walk very slowly home. We drive towards town and arrive at Pontis at 10.30, the right hour to start the evening. I ask Stavros if Marinos and his party had arrived. He looks at me oddly and calls Marinos over. Our tough-looking truck driver in the day has become a well-groomed waiter in the evening. Between serving us *meze*, a village salad and great chunks cut off the lamb on the spit, we discuss his great passion, his huge lorry.

"Mercedes?" I ask

"Yes."

"What speed?"

"50 kilometres"

"It's huge, how big?"

"It carries 26,500," he answers. I query the large number. "In Greece, some can take up to 40,000," which I translate into 40 tonnes. "But I carry that today," he says with a wicked grin.

It was just as well he didn't go flat out down the mountain.

A few minutes later, Stavros brings us another half litre of his potent red wine. "From Marinos," he says.

The evening is getting decidedly excellent. A deaf mute comes over to our table and leaves a plastic clock held up by two plastic dolphins, costing all of £3, according to his note in Greek and English. With my cheap watch having packed up, it is an offer I can't refuse. He gives me my change and goes off to do more trade. We then notice that he has left the £3 from another customer on the table. I catch up with him and his eyes speak a thank you which needs no words.

At midnight, with Pontis beginning to fill up, their happy old guitarist takes up an accordion, leaving his sombre partner on bass guitar. The tempo changes. A family celebrating their daughter's first birthday comes out onto the floor. They dance round in a circle from the grandfather to the little girl's two sisters, aged three and five. Fred had commented today on the Greeks needing to be civilised. This dance says it all. While we were savages in our loincloths, they were civilisation itself.

I think of Peter and Des coming in September with Sean. I hope we can dance together on their last night.

By now, it is half past the bewitching hour. I turn to see in the entrance a huge muscle man wearing just vest and shorts. It has to be Lefteris. He comes in with five of his mates, all dressed alike - bulging biceps and little else. We greet each other like old friends and they sit down. The bill had come, but I add six large beers and a hefty tip for Marinos. I go over to drink to the team's health and tell Lefteris's friends he is the best bulldozer driver in Greece.

"No, Nikos is the best. I am the second best," says Lefteris.

We all liked that and leave them to start their party. I am always surprised that Greeks can make merry all night and yet get to work in the morning. In England, the publican would have said "Last orders" some time ago. Here the taverna owner knows he is host and will go out of his way to make sure that everyone is happy and fed right up until the last person leaves. But for us, mere mortals, it is time for bed. Jannie and I creep out, and the Discovery crawls home.

Now it's the turn of the Land Rover. I slowly creep up the hill in first gear and stop. An eight point turn sees me round the hairpin bend and onto the terrace above.

Planning a party

Sunday 15 July, 32 down and 15 to go

Seriously hung over, I get up at 8.30 and open the shutters to see another glorious day in the making, with a still sea and Ortholithi reflected as in a mirror. We have an hour before the workers come. Today they will flatten the top terrace – but to where, I ask myself. I must mark out where the veranda will come and where we will build the retaining wall. After last night, if Lefteris feels the way I do, I can see him carving out the land until he gets right up to the house. With some difficulty, I stretch the string exactly three metres from the house.

I hear the clink of tea cups, Jannie is making breakfast.

"Do you realise what today is?" I ask her. "July 15 – we are already over two thirds the way through the project."

"July 15!" she cries. "You've forgotten; it is Louise's birthday."

We phone up our daughter and sing her "Happy birthday". I tell her about our evening out at Pontis, a taverna she has always loved, and how slow the progress has been.

"Don't worry, Daddy, I'll think of something," she says.

At exactly 9.30, Nikos Bulldozer and Lefteris arrive. Nikos's punctuality is unbelievable and it's a Sunday as well. They turn on the engines of their two monsters and let them idle to build up strength, while they plan the day.

Lefteris, with his Caterpillar, will do the big earth-moving; Nikos, with his JCB, will do the surgical work. Lefteris hacks into our sloping terrace and shoves the earth on top of the boxes. Old concrete pipes appear – the remains of the sewage system that fed the soakaway. From now on, we will use our emergency solution to sanitation – a mini Portaloo – a bucket, ostentatiously described as the chemical toilet.

Back and forward Lefteris drives, pressing down the earth with the huge weight of the Caterpillar until the land becomes concrete-hard.

Nikos meanwhile starts to attack the land in front of the olive tree terrace. His scoop is poised just above the historic rock, where my brother Peter and I stood thirty years ago, champagne in hand, celebrating the purchase of the land. I leap down to its defence. I have never taken on a JCB before. Nikos doesn't understand my sentimentality. As I turn my back to go up to the house, I hear an ominous crack. Nikos has now grabbed our dead oak and pulled it down. This has always been the boundary marker for the land and we planned to cut it down to two metres. At this rate Fred will be out of work. Nikos pulls it onto the now flattened terrace and plays pass the parcel with Lefteris. With a few shoves it is over the edge of the boxes to join the graveyard of the roses which also have met the end of a glorious and long life. Looking at the poplar tree above, I think - it's your turn next.

Lefteris carries on gouging under my directions. Nikos disappears and comes back with the JCB with the pneumatic drill. He now assaults the incredibly thick side wall to the property. He says he needs to cut it back so I can get the Land Rover through the gap he made in the corner box. What he really means is he wants it cut back so he can get the bulldozer down the hill. I am unhappy – I like the old wall. Another minor dispute starts. Lefteris comes over to give Nikos support. Suddenly Nikos leaps back from the JCB as it starts to emit a black spray. I have an ally. The poor machine has given up and has sprung an oil leak. They try and fix it but more oil spews out. The side wall remains more or less intact.

By now the land is level and it is time to measure how far we have gone down – it is 1.55 metres below the house. We discuss what to do next. Nikos wants to phone Pavlos, who will be building the retaining wall in front of the house and is meant to be here at 9.00 tomorrow. I decide that Nikos Mechanikos is a better source of inspiration and, at least, I can understand him. He is thrilled by the progess and tells Nikos Bulldozer to dig a trench for the foundations of the new wall. With this earth spread over the terrace and pressed down, we are still 1.50 metres below the veranda level, 15 cm below my marker and therefore 15 cm below where the pool will rest.

We sit down for some water and are joined by Nikos Builder, who is in great form. He has come to watch his friends work. He refuses my offer of water, pointing to his seriously extended stomach. "Eggs and bacon plus a litre of orange juice," he says in explanation. I reckon a loaf of bread as well.

I think the day is over, but Nikos Bulldozer wants to smooth out the road on the corner. This time he does the scooping and Lefteris follows with the flattening. We all admire the work.

Nikos Bulldozer says the road is ready for testing, so I go and get my car keys, but Nikos Builder beats me. He revs up his Honda mini-motorbike and, aiming for the hill which rises so steeply that his weight goes back, executes a perfect wheelie. He hurtles up to the corner and disappears in a cloud of dust. A second later, he appears again on the top terrace, triumphant. I could get to like this guy.

Now it's the turn of the Land Rover. I slowly creep up the hill in first gear and stop. I try to get going again but, to my embarrassment, the car won't move upwards. After some struggling I move into the lower set of gears and crawl forward again to the corner. An eight point turn sees me round the hairpin bend and onto the terrace above. Lefteris suggests I shouldn't try this after a night out at Pontis. A further seven point turn and I'm ready for the descent. With

Nikos Bulldozer on starboard look-out, Lefteris to port and Nikos Builder ahead, I retrace my steps.

We have a conference. Nikos Builder suggests I get a Suzuki 4x4 – he's obviously a Japanese fan. Nikos Bulldozer prefers to knock another metre off the boxes on the inside of the bend; he's a pneumatic drill fan. I suggest that when the road is surfaced we extend it out a metre from the outside wall; I fancy myself as a civil engineer. We agree to decide in September once the pool is in.

Before they leave, I look up the Greek word for hero in the dictionary. I announce that Nikos is a "Bulldozer *iroas* of the *Ellinikos Demokratia*". Everyone agrees and we part after a great victory.

Monday 16 July, 33 down and 14 to go

I awake to yet another glorious day. At 8.15 I buck up courage to phone Pavlos to tell him that Nikos is finished. Partner George answers Pavlos's mobile and promises a 9 o'clock start. The team, now five strong, arrives and marches up the new road.

"Good morning, John," says Pavlos. "Five coffees, please."

I show willingness to serve my men and turn to go into the kitchen. Pavlos grins, waves his finger and says what I assume was Greek for "only joking". The first job is to measure the trenches where the walls will go. We phone Nikos Mechanikos for the steel man's number, and Pavlos places his order.

This is going to be one of those good days. So I pop down to get some bread and a paper and boast about my new road. On my return I find my favourite Council workmen, Spiros Alamanos and son Alexandros, the community plumbers, are in the road. They are inspecting a kink in the mains pipe further up from the last break. Overnight, it has obviously got worse and all the water had left the pipe and gone down the road.

"It's that man again," says Alexandros, "he comes out at night and lifts the pipe over my pin and then lets all the water out."

I press him on the identity of the phantom pipe bender. At first he refuses to say; then he points up to Spiros, our neighbour on his bridge.

"But why?" I ask.

He points to the black patch above the burst pipe. "That's not water, it's shit. He allows the shit to come onto the road, then breaks the pipe so it washes away," he says.

Though I may not be Spiros's best friend, I felt that Alexandros might be going too far. But it's an interesting explanation.

It is time for breakfast, which gives Pavlos and his team an excuse for a short rest. A few minutes later, two go off to strip the wood off the road wall, while Pavlos, George Segal and the fifth man line up where the north wall will go. Conveniently there is a huge poplar half a metre outside the line so this will be the major support for the wooden frame.

George asks for something. This is becoming a habit; the client is supposed to have a stock of everything. So far I've found spades, bricks, pipes, iron bars and a mallet. Already this morning, they wanted a drill-bit for concrete but I didn't have one. He now indicates something long and thin.

"String?" I ask.

George rejects this. We go indoors, he points to the telephone line. I take him round the back of the house and point to a cable hanging from the roof, surplus to requirements. No, but I am getting warmer. We go back into the house and he points to the lead for the electric kettle. It then dawns on me: they want a long lead for their drill. Again I fail them.

In Greece, a builder carries a tape measure, a spirit level and his multi-purpose tool. The rest is found on site. The tool is a hammer on one side and a long claw on the other which the builder hangs over his shoulder, like a doctor's stethoscope. The claw has a curvaceous key hole in it; the smaller upper half is used for nail extraction, while the larger lower half is used to tighten the clamp which holds the sides of the wooden frame together. He also uses the hole to help turn steel. Finally he carries a bum bag full of nails, which he transfers one by one into his mouth while getting the wood into position. When in place, he takes the nail out of his mouth, flicks his wrist and stabs it into the wood. With one bang with the hammer, he's ready for the next plank. The claw can also be used as a mini pickaxe to clear the ground, and as a pencil to sketch his plans on any wall or floor at hand.

I phone Nikos Mechanikos to report progress. He is down in Lefkimmi. I ask him about the planning permission. It seems there are always problems at the mysterious Polodomia. Either the man is away or on strike or ill or cannot be found or at a funeral. He promises me to have another go today. I mention that the police haven't been. The road was one thing but walls up the top seem to be going too far with the story that I am only stabilising the land. He repeats his fears as well.

By now Pavlos and two have gone, leaving George and one to finish off. I ask when the steel will come.

"They cut it tomorrow and put it in on Wednesday," he answers.

"And you close the wall on Thursday and we pour the concrete on Friday?" I ask.

"Maybe," he says.

As he walks down the road to leave, I explain the problem of getting the Land Rover round the hairpin bend. I tell him that if we concrete the road, we could use the outer wall as the support for a concrete overhang to widen the road outwards instead of cutting the boxes on the inside of the bend. No problem, he says.

I phone Alexos Hirdaris to report good progress. He has already contacted Athens; he hopes the pool will come next Tuesday. I then remember he comes from the northeast of the island and would know where I could find Siniotic stone.

"Drive past Kassiopi and turn left to Nea Perithia where I live," he explains. There are further directions which I vaguely noted. As soon as we have a free moment we must venture into the mountains and buy stone.

Fred then phones and asks about coming on Saturday, an extra visit. Of the two poplars left, the one between the boxes and the slipped wall has already taken a hammering. It reduces the view of the sea and will drop its leaves into the pool. It has to go. The huge one at the north end of the terrace is too high to provide privacy from Spiros and will cause even more trouble for the pool. In the spring it generates cotton-like material and throughout the summer and autumn it sheds its leaves. It was also the main attraction of the millions of ants which Jannie reminded me was the cause of the old poplar falling down. If Nikos Mechanikos reckons cutting it down won't cause land problems, it should go as well. It will be a major challenge to drop it between the house and the new walls without damaging anything. If we are to cut it down we should do it before the pool comes; so I tell Fred we will be lumberjacks on Saturday.

Tuesday 17 July, 34 down and 13 to go

July in Corfu is hot. Today it is sticky as well. As the steel man hasn't arrived, I phone Nikos Mechanikos on his mobile. There's no reply, which is odd as he usually answers immediately whether he's in his BMW or on his moped. I phone Anna, his patient wife, who tells me he's left the mobile at home, so we decide to go into Corfu Town to look for Nikos. It is even hotter in town. We find him in his office.

"As the pool arrives next Tuesday, we need the steel tomorrow, so we can close the frame on Thursday and pour concrete on Friday," I explain. "Can we check that Pavlos has ordered it?"

"I'll phone my friend."

What I assumed would be an "*Avrio*? Yes or No" conversation, turns into a long discussion. My temperature begins to rise towards the forty degrees outside.

"We have a problem," says Nikos.

I'm fed up with problems; all I want is solutions. "So when do we get the steel?" I ask.

He shrugs his shoulders. "In two weeks time, maybe."

I explode: "Why?"

"Pavlos has given him the wrong instructions."

"You must be joking," I exclaim.

"No, but I'll send him a fax showing how I want the steel cut."

He then realises that I suffer from high blood pressure and am just about to blow a gasket.

"Don't worry, we can get the steel tomorrow or Thursday," he reassures me.

I leave a very unhappy man. I bitterly regret that I hadn't asked Nikos Mechanikos to check with the steel man after Pavlos had phoned through the measurements on Monday. We pick up Elena to see how Rob and Agalis's house is progressing. Someone is laying a wooden floor. We wander around the property; it looks as if a refuse vehicle has gone berserk. There is builder's rubbish everywhere.

Elena is almost in tears. "In a week's time the children arrive. The builders have had a year to complete the work and it is still not done. Everywhere you look there's a bit missing or a wall chipped," she says.

"What's the problem then?" I ask.

"The architect says he's artistic; maybe he is, but we pay him to manage the project. It's a complete mess."

Our solution to construction problems is to go for a swim on the east coast at Barbati, which had been our second choice thirty years ago when we were looking for land. In those days the beach was totally undeveloped, the only house being the three-storey red one in the south of the bay. Barbati's glory was the olive groves that came right down to the sea, giving shade from the summer sun. Remarkably the olive trees, huge like others across the island, are still there. Behind, however, for the whole length of the bay, is low level development – some of the houses attractive, others like chicken huts. The sea is as gorgeous as ever, although Elena says that on some days it can become polluted. I'm pleased we built on the west coast, which is washed by the open Mediterranean.

Wednesday 18 July, 35 down and 12 to go

The steel will arrive today, I think as I viewed the totally calm sea. But, I'd thought that yesterday. Before the sun comes over the mountain, I decide to do some hard labour. After the workmen have been, it's a litter pick. Today, I move the surplus steel from building the road up to the new terrace, where it can reinforce the veranda retaining wall. Dragging a couple of five metre rods up the road is hard work, but it passes the time before the steel team arrives.

Eventually, at 10.30, a small flat bed truck stops below. The good news is that it's weighed down with steel; the bad news that Spiros, the driver, is alone.

He backs up the new road a few metres, tilts the back of his pick-up down as far as it will go and moves forward to release the load. Unfortunately, the road is so steep that the steel won't slip off the back. No problem. Spiros gets out of his cab, clambers on to the steel and, lifting bundles of a dozen rods at a time, hurls them over the side. Spiros was a true Olympian. So I told him so.

"No English," he starts, in English.

From then on it is a mixture of Greek for Beginners and sign language for the deaf. Here was someone who wanted to talk. "Don't worry; they will fix the steel tomorrow," he says.

I explain that it has taken me four weeks to build the wall.

"I make my wall in April, May, June, July and maybe August, September," says Spiros. It seems that he has even more problems than me.

"Are you from Corfu?" I ask.

"No, from Athens. I marry woman from Corfu."

"Are the building problems the same in Athens?"

He ignores my question, but says: "In Corfu, men don't work; they," rubbing his enormous girth, "eat *pastistada* and", jigging around, "dance."

He was worth a coffee.

"No sugar, no milk, black," he says.

"Cold?"

He thinks I'm mad. "Of course."

He comes up to discuss life. He is on the stage, the terrace where the pool will go, and I am in the dress circle, the terrace where the veranda will be.

"Corfu is very beautiful?" I suggest.

With a dramatic sweep of his monstrous arm he shows me the sea and replies, "Lo, behold, beautiful sea."

"Can you swim?" I ask him.

Huge roar. "No." Hand facing down, he demonstrates a rock falling to the bottom of the sea.

"Do you have children?" I enquire.

"Boy and girl. Boy very strong," he says, rippling his biceps.

"Olympics?" I suggest.

He waddles across the stage, "very slow," but perks up, "good in sea."

As he leaves he reminds me of the Corfiots, "*pastistada* and dance".

I phone Nikos Mechanikos with the good news. "We can put up the steel tomorrow? Then close the wall on Friday and then pour the concrete on Monday?" I ask.

"John, I tell you always, you cannot have a programme. No more of this 'then' and 'then'."

138

I agree to phone Pavlos to get the next job done. I have no problems with this so long as it is one-way conversation, but I still have problems with his replies. So I turn to our support in troubled times, George Texaco.

He agrees to phone Pavlos.

Pavlos offers to come late Thursday morning and, following the steel men as they erect the cage inside, construct the wooden frame. By Friday morning they would have closed the whole wall and they could pour from three o'clock. If this programme works, I'm for programmes.

Now we go on to our accountant, Amalia – our favourite person in Corfu. I tell her about the progress since the last time we saw her two weeks before.

"We have a fine road up to the house; the bulldozer can get up, but we can't."

She thinks this is hilarious; we are definitely her favourite clients.

"Have you had any progress in changing the ownership from the company to ourselves?" I ask.

"No, I've been on holiday," she replies.

If ever anyone deserves a holiday it's Amalia.

"It's worse when you get back," I suggest, "even more work to do?"

As if to a fellow conspirator, she hooks her index finger for me to look on the floor behind her desk. There I see four large plastic supermarket bags, full of invoices and receipts.

"And how many companies is that?"

"Twenty-two," she answers, laughing slightly hysterically. The Greeks are probably better at making paper than pouring concrete and they are very good at doing that even if it is never on time. The greatest gripe mentioned by the workers is always the enemy – the bureaucracy. The answer is a large envelope. Everything will finish in there and will be passed to the poor accountant. Nowadays every person, as well as every trader, has a tax code. It will be Amalia's job to draw up their accounts ready for the taxman. At least, the country is fighting the people's great antipathy to paying their taxes.

We leave her to get on with her work. To complete an excellent day, I decide it is time to have a chat with Nikos Builder. He is on his mobile.

"I'll see you at nine this evening," he says.

Corfu in July can be very hot even without the hassle of building. Jannie decides that, before returning to the battleground, we need an ice-cream. We use only the colonnaded roads to cross the Old Town to *Mourayia*, the 'walled' area which sits on cliffs above the sea. Today we don't play our game of trying to get lost amongst the maze of narrow alleys, which always amazes our friends. We sit down at Andranik's, the café of the Armenian refugee who arrived in the early 1920s. It still makes the best ice-cream on the island. We relax and watch the boats go by.

"Have you noticed the name of that ferry line?" asks Jannie.

"Fast Ferries," I reply.

"And Minoan has its High Speed Ferries," she says; then she pauses. "And there's the Superfast Ferry that passes to the west of Corfu." With a great smile she then adds: "I wish we could find Superfast Wall Builders."

I think about this excellent idea and then see the similarity. "The ferries and the builders are the same. The ferries are boarding up until the last moment before departure; the builders are working right up to their deadline."

"That's because the Greeks are always turning up for the ferry with only minutes to spare. It's their unique way of life – they expect everything to happen at the last moment," she adds.

I laugh as she has defined the perfect analogy. "But what happens when you want to buy a ticket on Fast Ferries for the next day? Do you remember? We couldn't; they said that they only sell tickets for same day's boats."

"That's because of the bureaucracy," she replies. "It's rather like getting a piece of paper from the planning office – impossible."

The view north from Corfu Town is splendid. There, across the bay, is Pantocrator, the highest mountain on the island and home to our stone.

"As we have the afternoon free, let's go for a trip north," suggests Jannie.

We crawl along the corniche past Barbati, Nissaki to Kouloura. All the way, tourist buses are nose to tail – it is truly a gorgeous trip above numerous little bays. On we go past Kassiopi and then turn left up to Nea Perithia and we are lost. Without my dictionary to tell me the word for 'quarry', I am reduced to asking the few who are not asleep: "Where is the stone?" It is an inane question in an area where everything is stone. We climb higher and eventually find where the mountainside has been blasted out. Huge machines are idle – even they are having their siesta. A solitary man sits on a large stone by the entrance.

"Can I buy some stone?" I ask.

"How many cubic metres do you want?"

"I don't know. Can you deliver it to Agios Gordis?"

He obviously reckons his visitor is an idiot. "No, you come and get it yourself," he replies. He looks at the Land Rover and thinks, at first, I want just a few rocks. I correct him, so he wanders off to a hut and returns brandishing a piece of paper on which he has written his telephone number. We discuss the price of a cubic metre, which sounds like a lot of stone at a very reasonable cost, and shake on what seems an excellent deal.

Before leaving we look north, across the sea, to Agii Saranda and Albania. For one who is biased towards the west coast, I have to admit that up here, amongst the eagles, is a view even more dramatic than ours. Before returning home we drive higher up into the mountains and find derelict villages, hidden in valleys, to which the people on the coast moved to be out of view from the sea, when marauding pirates had terrorised the island. Later, more people moved in to escape from the malaria-carrying mosquitoes that bred in the marshes and lagoons by the sea. In the poor pastures of this barren land they tended their livestock, which during the war was confiscated by the Germans. The men left to fight and the villages became uninhabited. Now beautiful old houses are being restored and summer visitors come to enjoy the coolness and the peace high above the crowded beaches.

We make our way home to meet Nikos Builder, who arrives as he promised. We discuss sewage pipes and drains, electricity for the pool, the jardinière and its wall, which will be to the north of the concrete wall we are now building, and finally his schedule. I show him my diary. We will be in England for five weeks till early September. No problem – all will be finished when we return. What a wonderful man, maybe he should have done the twenty-five metres of wall we are now building.

We then come to my new problem – the stone. "Can you put stone on the concrete walls," I ask.

"Of course. My Albanian is an expert at breaking stone," he replies.

I envisage someone who has spent a few years in Enver Hoxha's jail.

"We've seen some near Nea Perithia. Can you get it?"

"No problem. Nikos Bulldozer will get the Mercedes truck up there and bring it back."

I give him the telephone number and tell him the price I am paying, which is far too high in his eyes. As he leaves, I turn to Jannie and express our joint view: "With Nikos Builder and Nikos Bulldozer, we can only succeed."

Chicken and a half-litre of wine at Georgy Porgy's is a fitting end to the day. Nikos Builder comes by to get a take-away and as he says goodnight, another half-litre arrives at our table. Georgy Porgy points to Nikos when I suggest I hadn't ordered it. We stroll through the dark streets of our ancient village, with a glorious star-lit night above. Corfu, I love you.

Thursday 19 July, 36 down and 11 to go

To be woken up by workmen means either too much wine the night before or an early start for the steel men. It is a bit of both. At 8.30, two young muscle-men in white T-shirts arrive with an older man, and someone I at first think is very old indeed. They carry up steel rods, seven at a time, and then ask to borrow my spade to clear the base of the earth which had crumbled from the sides. I was expecting to lend them something.

Two work on the north and west walls, ten metres in total, while the other two start at the south end of the fifteen metre east wall, which will hold up the veranda, and move north to meet eventually the other team. Cross rods, then vertical rods, complete the back. The bottom of the base is installed, followed by the front and the top of the base.

After a few attempts to make conversation in Greek, I find out that they are all from Corfu Town, except for the "elderly" man, Mike, who is from Dassia. Mike, who turns out to be only fifty-two, is suntanned to a mature leather colour and peers out from indented eyes below overlapping bushy eyebrows. He is lean and walks with arms hanging outwards, rather ape-like. In total, he is not a pretty sight. However, his English is more than passable and he is out to prove that looks aren't everything. He lived for six months in England, at what sounds like Felixstowe, though he claims it was five hours from London by train and ten by car – this being in the good old days before stationary motorways and privatised railways.

"Were you on the boats?" I ask him, as this is where most Greeks learn their English.

"No," he pauses, "*padremenos*," "I'm married" – he has forgotten the English word.

143

My conversations always start with: where do you live, are you married and have you any children?

"My home is empty, my wife has flown," he says, demonstrating this by flapping his arms. "She lives in England with my three daughters," he adds sadly, repeating a story one hears too often.

Mike has a natural command of what is going on, so I ask him if he is the *Efendikos*, the boss.

Great laughter and he points to the serious one, "£2,000 a week, big car, five wives," he says. *Efendikos* explains that Mike is mad and drinks too much wine, another familiar story.

It is time to phone Pavlos to tell him the good news: we are making excellent progress and he can come over and start closing the walls. A message on the phone tells me we haven't paid our bill, so the telephone is cut off except for emergencies. In my view this is an emergency, so we have to go into town to pay a fine. As Greece is a cash society, we have an endless queue to find out what the fine is, then an endless queue to get money out of the bank, then an endless queue to make the payment; it all takes ages.

We rush home. The steel men have finished but there is still no Pavlos. I phone him from the public call box in the valley, after waiting in another queue, and we have another one-sided conversation. He promises to close the walls tomorrow, and may pour the concrete if he has time.

Faced with yet another missed weekend, I think: do I phone Nikos Mechanikos, whose contacts with Pavlos are infrequent and probably not very friendly, or George Texaco, who has already got the promise out of Pavlos to come today? George, who is fixing a car, says he will phone Pavlos and get back to me. I decide to contact Nikos as well. He's at the Polodomia. He'll phone back at 2.00 when he is in the office. He doesn't, so I go down to the valley and phone again.

"He's on his mobile," says Spiros Zervos.

He isn't. I then phone George who tells me that Pavlos blames the steel men who should have done the work yesterday and that he will close the wall tomorrow and pour the concrete on Monday. I am resigned to the inevitable and wonder if the Athenians with our prefabricated pool will do any better.

A siesta puts a new light on the world. A cup of tea and some writing under the olive tree adds to the pleasure. The sun shimmers on the sea below; who cares about walls? Suddenly the phone rings: obviously the Greeks are good at reconnecting phone lines. Our daughter Louise is as enthusiastic as ever.

"Daddy, when you phoned me on my birthday, I promised I'd think about your problems. I have just had a fantastic idea," she says, sounding like her father. "In Peter Mayle's book, *A Year in Provence*, he invites the families of all the workmen to a party to be held when the work is to be finished. The workers can't lose face, so the work is done. Why don't you do the same?"

Minutes later, Nikos Mechanikos phones. "I've talked to Proskyr, they will pour the concrete tomorrow, but only when they know that Pavlos is finished," he says. "Can we get Pavlos to finish?"

"Please phone him," I beg.

"Every time I phone him, he doesn't do what he says," replies Nikos.

"Every time I phone him, I don't even know what he says," I counter.

"But I have phoned him a thousand times."

"Please, for me, Nikos, phone him once more; ask him to come at 7.30." I then add, "You must hate the day you met me."

"Yes, yes!"

I think he's joking, but perhaps he isn't.

Nikos phones back a few minutes later. "He's agreed. We'll phone the concrete people in the morning."

"Bravo, Nikos. What do you think of having a party when all the work is done?"

"Fantastic idea."

Jannie thinks he says fantastic because he likes sitting under the olive tree eating lunch with us. It is two hours from sunset, so we decide on an early swim. We start down the road to the beach, when a large black Mercedes pulls up.

"I'll give you a lift," says Michael from the Romantic View.

"Thanks," says Jannie, who is better going uphill than down. I prefer going downhill than up.

I tell Michael about my ideas for a party.

"We don't do that in Greece," he replies. It appears that the last thing on earth he would like to do is have a party with the workers. "Greek workers are all the same, John. The engineer says a wall will need ten cubic metres of concrete and the builder then says he's used twenty. So I complain and they down tools and walk off."

"I must be lucky, as I didn't have that problem with my wall," I say.

"I saw Nikos Builder at your home when I was leaving," he says. "I have had problems with him not turning up when he said he would."

"But he's there for us today as he promised."

He's not impressed. "Greeks always turn up punctually on the first day. It's later on that you have a problem when they take on new business. But maybe you'll be OK in August, since there's no work to do on the hotels."

We have our swim and then amble back up to see how Nikos Builder is getting on.

I am worried. My plan was to take the main sewage pipe out from the house, under the veranda terrace, through its retaining wall into the open space under the surrounds of the pool, in case we needed to get access. From there it would go outside the retaining wall and meet up with the pipes from the extension bathrooms. Nikos instead has laid the pipe on the house side of the retaining wall, under where my beautiful terracotta tiled terrace will be. At the corner he has put a plastic chimney the size of the hole on a golf green which will stick through my terrace. Beside the house, he has left the huge pit where sewage gathered when the old pipes broke. So now we will have a manhole in the terrace as well. He assures me he can make the pit smaller and fit a 25x25 cm cover the same size as a tile. I'm less than happy. We now follow the sewage pipe towards where he will build the extension. He explains that this is where he will build another manhole.

"But that's in the bedroom," I explain.

"Don't worry; we can lay the pipe under the outside wall."

It is too late to say that this is why I wanted to go through the retaining wall first. That'll teach me to be away when the builder comes. Is this a foretaste of things to come when we are in England?

By now, the sun is setting.

"John, Nikos Bulldozer is bringing the stone this evening," announces Nikos Builder. "He is rather late, but I am sure he'll be here soon."

Twenty minutes later as the sky darkens, we hear, from the top of the mountain, a low whine followed every ten seconds by a hissing – the unmistakable sound over an overloaded Mercedes crawling down the road from Sinarades in its lowest gear with the brakes being applied intermittently. Nikos Bulldozer halts above us and calls down that he will drop his load over the huge wall that holds up the road. Having seen a truck load of wooden planks and posts successfully land on the shelf on which the house stands, I am totally confident in our hero. I go inside, however, in case anything goes wrong.

There is an almighty roar as forty tonnes of rock falls onto our land. I then hear high pitched screams coming from Spiros next door. I look out but cannot see my neighbour's house for the huge cloud of dust that is rising. As the screams continue, I call up to Nikos Bulldozer to go and find out what has happened. A few minutes later he comes over from next door to explain that one of Spiros's guests is having a fit.

"She thinks there's been an earthquake and a great landslide has nearly killed her," says Nikos. "And Spiros says he must take her to hospital because she has broken her arm."

"And has she?" I ask.

"Not that I can see. Anyway Spiros has told me that he is going to sue me."

"Don't worry, Nikos," I say reassuringly. "The best lawyer on the island, Konstantinos Socrates Tsivanides, will defend you. And I will pay."

The two Nikoses leave in triumph; and we have our stone.

Friday 20 July, 37 down and 10 to go

Today will be the big battle. Will Pavlos come? I think he will. Will he be here at 7.30? Well, miracles do happen.

I look out to sea: it is silver. There are dark patches where a gentle breeze is rippling the surface. A white yacht motors along one of the grey roads that cross the wakening sea; they could be rivers of warmer water. A rustle in the poplars warns of a coming wind. The tops of the olive trees gently sway while the tips of the cypresses stand firm. The sea merges into the sky, with the horizon drawn by a thin white fluffy line of sea fog.

The time for battle arrives and passes. Five minutes later, I hear the crack of spinning tyres below and see dust appearing over the boxes. Pavlos has arrived. He backs a few metres up the track which is our road. A head appears, grey haired and smiling; it's Pavlos, himself. George Segal follows.

"Good morning, John."

With one other worker, they walk over to the steel frame which they must cover with wood, the closing of the wall. They talk, perhaps critically, of its construction. I don't wait for the "there's a problem" comment and make for the kitchen to make coffee. I'm better at that.

George, elegantly turned out in white T-shirt, white socks and matching pale beige shorts and trainers, is the middleweight to Pavlos's lightweight. He sees a pile of unused steel bars in the olive trees below and brings them up. He obviously feels that the steel frame should be stronger. He places the corner of a rod into the mouth of his cutting machine, a sort of overgrown branch lopper. With one of its arms on the ground, he uses the other as a bar to vault on, high up into the air. As he comes down to earth the arm descends and the mouth cuts the rod in half. Pavlos and mate, with the skill of the best steel man, stitch a third mesh on the cage. This will obviously give the wall more strength and use up surplus steel.

An hour later, Pavlos moves from steel to wood. With great skill and speed they finish the ten metres of the west wall and move on to the north wall facing Spiros. The phone goes.

"How's it going?" asks Nikos Mechanikos.

"Very well," I reply, telling him of progress.

"Get Pavlos to estimate the amount of concrete he needs when he's finished the north wall."

An hour later, Nikos phones again and I tell him our estimate is twenty-six cubic metres, over three lorry loads of ready-mix concrete, even more than for the road wall.

"Bad news, John," he says, "Proskyr cannot pour the concrete today - they are full."

"Can they pour tomorrow?" I ask.

"No, they never work weekends. They also said they can't pour on Monday. So I told them we will get someone else. Now they've agreed to be with you on Monday at 12."

As it turns out, I had underestimated the amount of work Pavlos and his team have to do. One of the team spends the day in our neighbour's olive grove retrieving the wood they had taken off the road wall. The Greeks believe that the land next door is better than the land they are working on to throw rubbish, wood, anything and everything. Our wood retriever

149

is amused that I am watching him climb up through the olives and over a terrace with eight three metre planks on his shoulder.

"How many can you carry?" he asks.

"Only three," I reply.

"But you are twice my age."

By two o'clock, the wood erectors have overtaken the wood retriever and leave, promising to come *avrio*. In fact, Pavlos goes next door and spends two hours removing nails from the timber used for the road wall. Maybe my neighbour will need some nails one day.

The great glory of the west coast is its moods. From a gentle start of the day, the wind has grown in strength and now its wildness has come. Right across the bay, waves roll in, beating themselves on the shore. The sandbanks break their majestic rhythm and turn them into frothing dragons. To the meek, the beach is the safest place. To the brave, the dive deep though the breakers, under the rushing water, is rewarded by a lonely sea, one moment low with the beach out of sight, the next moment high as watchers came back into view. The return to land offers danger, either the tumble over the breaking wave, which throws the unwary to the bottom, or the body surf in over protruding rocks and finally the attempt to stand in the shallows as the water sucks the unstable down the coast to a painful landing.

Fotis and Tassos watch. Unlike others on the beach who are driven by money, their restaurant offers them the most perfect spot to just exist. The taverna hasn't changed much since we first came thirty-five years ago. The concrete tables are from another world. The roof is unchanged: why change it if it keeps out the rain? I think they do nothing because that would be a hassle.

"You promised to shave if the work progresses," Tassos reminds me, "and you are very unshaven tonight."

"On Monday, we will pour more concrete and the walls around the pool will be finished. The Athenians then come on

Tuesday with the pool. I'll shave then and we'll all celebrate."

"We know what Greek workers are like – they'll never finish."

"But we are going to motivate them, we'll have a party when they finish."

Motivation is not a word in his vocabulary, but he understands enough to be very worried. "John, don't do that, we don't have parties with the workers in Greece."

We leave depressed.

Saturday 21 July, 38 down and 9 to go

We breakfast under the great olive tree, but there is no sign of Pavlos. At times like this one must be philosophical. *Avrio* is *Avrio* and today is the weekend. The Greeks never worry so why should we. Everything is *siga, siga*, slowly, slowly. On Monday, Pavlos will come early and finish before the concrete arrives.

Nikos Builder has agreed to pay for tiles and fittings for the extension, so we feel it is our birthday. We can choose what we want, so off we go past the Parelion Council Offices and left along the Ropa Valley to Ideal Standard. How anyone would choose this location for a showroom is a mystery. Standing alone in the empty valley with little passing traffic seems a recipe for financial disaster. We are met by a young happy man who wants to show us everything. Of course he is another Nikos, so the omen is good.

Why does age make couples compatible? In our youth, Jannie and I couldn't agree on anything. Now we agree instantly on wall and floor tiles for a bedroom and two bathrooms plus everything that goes in the bathrooms. Maybe it's because the choice is limited, the quality is excellent and Nikos is a born salesman. His father, Spiros, is very proud of his son, particularly as he speaks English. Nikos, however, is more proud of his motor bike, whose engine is so large that no road on the island can cope with its power.

On our way home we visit George Texaco at his garage. Caroline is in favour of a party. "We had a party when we opened the garage," she says. "All our future clients came."

"Well, we are opening a pool," I venture. "But I'm not sure if I want all the workers to take that as a signal that they can come and swim."

"Let's hope we can make it," says George. "Under the new law, the garage closes alternate weekends, so there's a 50:50 chance we will come."

"You are different; you are friends not workers." I then refer to their son, who is the same age as our eldest grandson. "Both of you and Panayiotis are welcome to come and swim at any time."

Back home we are met by a real surprise. A truck and a car are parked up our track. Pavlos, George Segal and two wood men are there, hard at work. George, the more forthcoming of the partners, plays back my favourite Greek phrase.

"Where have you been?" he asks. "We have been waiting."

They have been there since ten o'clock so I feel a bit guilty: they are missing their coffee.

"Pavlos, the good news," I say. He's very attentive, waiting for some appalling Greek to follow. I get out the dictionary. "*Party*, Pavlos." The word is the same in Greek.

"Where? When?" Pavlos asks.

"Here, September 9th," I reply.

"Why?"

"Because all the work will be finished. OK?" His smile confirms his answer. "A little beer, a little wine" I add.

"And a little ouzo?" asks Pavlos.

"Yes, and a little swimming."

This obviously appeals to Pavlos as he laughs and pulls down his shorts to reveal a white bottom. He walks up and down, waggling at everyone. I suddenly have second thoughts about the party.

Just as they did for the road walls below, they tighten up the locks on the cross rods between the two sided wooden frames on both the west and the north walls. With the retaining wall next to the house, there is a different problem. The wooden frame is only on one side of the steel. The other side is the excavated land. To support the frame they need to create flying buttresses along the length of the wall by driving thick two metre posts into the terrace to act as supports.

At this point, Nikos Builder turns up. He and George Segal are raising their voices, a common but not alarming practice in Greece. They are debating Nikos's masterpiece, the pipe out from the existing manhole to the retaining wall and then along its length. I interrupt them by telling Nikos about the party. I emphasise that we would only have it if everything is finished and the pool is full. Nikos, who totally understands my English, turns to Pavlos and repeats the conditions. I think Nikos likes doing this; he's the top dog now - he understands what the Englishman says. I hope the penny has dropped. All is finished by 3, so it's siesta time.

Living on the west coast of Corfu has its advantages. When construction schedules are not ruling us, our days can start late as we are in the shadow of the mountain, but they will go on later as each day we follow the sun over the horizon before the night's entertainment starts. On the east coast in the winter, they lose their sun by mid afternoon and the cold evenings close in early. We, on the other hand, can soak up every ray of warmth the lowly sun will give us. In the summer, we can swim off our empty beach as the sun is going down and then drink a glass of wine before venturing out.

Tonight, we are treating ourselves to something special. In the village of Kastellani Messis, once capital of the central area of the island, the *messis*, a traditional two-storey stone house hides one of Corfu's best kept secrets. Only after ten in the evening does the casual visitor realise that this is no villager's home but a setting for great eating and great listening. A quarter of the top floor has been cut away to make a mezzanine on which four small tables just fit and from where there is a view of two guitarists in the far corner. Downstairs a further six tables are assembled according to the parties that have booked – and without a booking, there is no access on a Saturday night. Our taverna has two names: *Musikomezedopolio*, 'the musical, meze shop', or *Filaki*, the jail.

Spiros, the owner and Maitre d', explains, in Greek, what *meze* is on offer, there is no menu. In some way, a twosome is wasted here. A party would order every dish and then share it. Tonight there are the standard choices, which we would normally be happy with, but we can have them elsewhere. However, it is the chicken pie, that Jannie knows Spiros always has, that makes her evening.

I separate guitarists into two camps: those that strum chords and those that pluck notes. Tonight it is the intricate finger work that enchants the guests. We are treated to a classical concert rather than the 'knees-up' of other tavernas. Their fine baritone voices are added to the quality of their playing. By midnight, with tables all taken and overflowing with plates that will be savoured as the night goes on, we move to what makes the evening unique. Spiros joins the duo and sings the softest of ballads in a perfect tenor, almost counter-tenor, voice.

The music stops and our host starts to tell jokes; the audience laughs; we are confused. It is at that moment that I know I should have kept up my Greek lessons. Spiros then visits each table and the laughter continues. He joins us and, in appalling Greek I tell him my Kastellani story: how in 1970 we had drunk a perfect red wine labelled 'Kastellani 1969'; in each of the following years we had found bottles with the same label but of varying colour and quality; and how our engineer had then explained that someone had obviously printed too many labels. I sense a nervous smile – perhaps he thinks my comment was about his wine. In response, as perhaps a peace offering, the customary half-litre on the house is proffered, accepted and drunk – what else can we do?

On our way home we ask ourselves: where, but here in Corfu, would we find such pleasure?

By 11.00, the pool panels are fitting and the struts are in place
    "Three hours to go, Valdek," I announce.
    "No problem. Two cafés frappés please," he replies.
    They deserve them. Christos, the non-coffee drinking
Albanian, carries on bolting the panels together. Christos
the Pole meanwhile gets out the theodolite and checks up on
the topless girls on the beach.

Installing the pool

Monday 23 July, 40 down and 7 to go

Lying in bed planning is easier than getting up and doing. The plan for our last week before returning to England is simple. Today at 12.00, we pour the concrete for the outer walls. Tomorrow we remove the wood and, in the afternoon, the pool men come from Athens. On Wednesday Nikos Bulldozer digs the deep end. By the end of the week we'll have our plastic pool. Then we can brief everyone on what to do when we are away. On our return we will put the liner in the pool. Nothing can go wrong, can it?

Suddenly I am aroused by a noise from outside. I blearily look out; there are four men. One says in English. "We are here."

I think; that's obvious, but who are you? Only on a third look do I recognise Alexos, the pool engineer.

"The pool is here," he says; "they've brought it on the overnight ferry from Patras."

In Greece nothing ever comes on the correct day; it's either the day after or the day before. The three Athenians, in shorts and T-shirts, are young. I sense they are here for a holiday. One of them looks far below to the beach. Without a 'how do you do' he goes into house, appearing seconds later with the binoculars. He's seen a topless sunbather. He passes the binoculars around. Moments later, a young couple comes out onto a balcony at Spiros's next door. They are in a hot embrace. All eyes turn; our Athenians are going to have some fun this week.

I turn to the oldest, a strapping blond over six feet tall. On the end of his chin he has a beard which grows up to the middle of his mouth over which hair is sprouting, indicating the start of a moustache.

"What's your name?" I ask.

"I'm Valdek."

"That's not a Greek name?"

"No, I'm from Poland," he says.

"*Gin dobrey*," I reply. I'm a great believer in learning a little in many languages – and that was the little I knew in Polish. "And the others?"

Introducing a tall clean shaven blond, he says: "Christos is also from Poland." Pointing to the swarthy, stocky and short one, he continues: "He's also Christos, from Albania."

Alexos now goes into the technical issues. "Where will the pool be?" he asks.

I point to some markers on the new terrace.

"No problem, where will we get the electricity?"

I point to the end of the retaining wall where we will build the extra bedroom.

"No problem, where will the cover be?"

Again no problem and so it goes on. It seems the outlet pipe from the pool is also no problem until Valdek joins in. He thinks the best solution is to siphon the water off. "Is that OK?" he asks.

"No problem," I reply, without telling him that I am an expert, having siphoned water out of the soakaway, much to the consternation of our councillor from down the hill.

The important matter of where they stay is next on the agenda. I volunteer to go down to the valley to ask advice of George and Nellie, who run the supermarket on the corner.

"Are they young and handsome?" Nellie asks.

"Of course, Nellie," I reply.

"In which case, they can stay with me."

Sharing my alarm, George suggests that Spiridoula, who runs Pandora's Box, might help. It turns out that she is the sister of George Texaco. It's a small world. She luckily has some vacant rooms.

Back at the house, Alexos Hirdaris has phoned Proskyr to order his concrete for Wednesday and confirms that ours will arrive at 12.30 today. Nikos Bulldozer has been summoned to discuss the excavation of the deep end of the pool. He comes on his Bulldozer, with his moped in the scoop, all ready for action. He is surprised that the wall has not been finished but, knowing Pavlos's performance, is pleased that we pour today. He reckons we can remove the wood tomorrow so that he can do his digging in the afternoon. Just as he is leaving I tell him the good news.

"I know, the party," he replies. News gets around very quickly.

The pool men go off to find their lodgings and we wait for the pump. It arrives at one and Pavlos turns up as well. One of his men starts watering the wooden frame. It seems that everything to do with walls needs watering. By now the pump has started pouring the concrete. It stops. Something is wrong. They go back to the monster which has got a load of concrete stuck somewhere up its neck. They check each part and find a gaping hole in one of the huge metal pipes. The pressure required to burst it must have been enormous. Nikos the Pump, who controls the machine, and the driver of the pre-mix concrete lorry hammer at the five metre tube until it is loose and then pull it out. They measure it and phone for a replacement. I had thought that this would be a good day. Now we have Pavlos and his team of four plus three Athenians, all waiting for action. Nobody cares; they happily sit under the olive trees and talk.

The phone goes. It's Nikos Mechanikos. I tell him my good news – we are pouring concrete and the pool has arrived. He then tells me his good news. The permit will be signed and dated today. We are legal.

The phone goes again. Our solicitor in Deal has finalised the sale of the flat; so we have money to pay for the pool and the extension. What timing!

It's 4.30 and George Segal and one mate have gone, leaving Pavlos and the other to do a four man job. With the pump now working they pour the concrete into the frame until it oozes out of the bottom. They stop pumping, and then one rakes the concrete while the other smooths it with a trowel. Pavlos screams for water as the concrete is drying too quickly. Pump, rake, smooth, water, pump, rake, smooth, water: the race goes on. As the concrete starts to rise up the frame, the raking and smoothing are replaced by creaming and hammering. The mate forces air into the concrete with his creamer and Pavlos bangs at the side of the frame with a post. He then gets a three metre plank to drive the concrete lower. This is more than theatre; it is the Naked Chef making a soufflé, an omelette, a salad and mayonnaise at the same time.

"*Opa*" or "*Allay*" calls Pavlos, and Nikos the Pump sends up more concrete. A whistle and he stops.

In the battle to fill the north wall, the neck of the pump gets entangled with the huge poplar, which we will have to cut back. The mate calls for a saw and shins up the tree – "just like a monkey" says Pavlos – and cuts off the bough. At this rate Fred will be redundant. With the third lorry empty, Nikos Pump phones through for a final six cubic metres, twenty-six in all.

"*Finito basta*?" I ask in my pidgin Italian; older Corfiots learnt it during the occupation.

"*Finito musica, finito fiesta!*" replies Pavlos.

Pavlos and his mate sit under the shade of the poplar tree, washing concrete off themselves. Below, the concrete lorry is also being washed down so that no ready-mix is left in the spout that delivers its load.

At 7.30, the last lorry arrives. Pavlos again waters everything. They start up the pump again. Nothing happens, and then from the trunk comes a hissing and at last a vast solid turd, before the wet concrete starts flowing again. The mate hammers and Pavlos pours like a maniac with an out-of-control elephant. He sees me watching and points to the hose. "*Nero,*" he orders, and I spray water randomly over any concrete I see.

Nikos the Pump calls over that we are now into our last cubic metre. Pavlos and mate rush along the terrace, Pavlos pouring and the mate digging with my spade against the wooden frame. Concrete is everywhere: on the wall of the house, on the shutters, on the windows and above all on Pavlos. From being just grey haired, he has become grey all over. I offer him a shower but his mate grabs the hose and gives him one on the terrace. We all laugh. The job is done.

Yiannis from Proskyr turns up with the paperwork and the pump regurgitates the last remnants of the concrete from its trunk, its neck and finally from its mouth with the meat-mincer teeth and mesh.

We get ready for a swim. Nikos Mechanikos phones. He cannot believe everything is finished and tomorrow we start installing the pool.

"With your organization, we have a programme; with mine at the polothomia, we have a permit," he says jubilantly.

Shimmering sea, here we come and then on to Georgy Porgy's to celebrate. I'll shave in the morning, maybe.

Tuesday 24 July, 41 down and 6 to go

I am now the expert wall waterer. All is complete by 7.30 when Pavlos arrives for breakfast under the olive tree. He's in a good mood nowadays and offers me a coffee – he had picked up some on his way to work. Soon he is joined by George Segal and the rest of the team. They destroy their wooden masterpiece quicker than they built it. The all-purpose hammer, claw, rod bending, pickaxe tool is now used to strip off the nails and bits of concrete that have adhered to the wood.

I shave. George says "beautiful". I thought he meant the wall; I'm worried – he doesn't; he's pointing at me.

The Athenians are bringing up to base-camp vast quantities of material: numerous tool boxes, flex, plastic bags with Wellington boots and sandals, a pool hose, rolls of blue liner, buckets of chemicals, rods of all shapes and sizes, aluminium strips, two long stainless steel tubes and the prize, the filter block. This contains the pump, filtration plant, pool light, steps and platform which our daughter's children will use as a diving board.

Down by the road are twelve black plastic panels, 2 metres long and 1.35 metres deep. Four of them are bent at right angles, the other eight are straight. Each is about 25 centimetres thick, with one side corrugated for strength and the other smooth for the inside of the pool. These will be assembled 15 centimetres off the ground after Nikos Bulldozer has dug the deep end. He's due at three o'clock.

The last piece of equipment is a theodolite. I'm impressed. It is the first I have seen on Corfu. Valdek, the boss, is using it to look at girls on the beach.

It's time to pay Pavlos.

"Good news, Pavlos. I have dollars," I tease him.

The six others turn round. Pavlos exclaims: "Dollars?" He pulls out one pocket, empty. He pulls out the other and throws a few drachmas to the ground. All cheer. He puts his hands out for the dollars and I give him a bundle of drachmas.

Everyone cries: "We want dollars."

We discuss the number of cubic metres of concrete. Pavlos says 25, Proskyr 26. Pavlos is happy to be paid for 25 and tells me to sort out Proskyr.

We go to town to collect more money from the bank and wait thirty minutes in a queue. One counter clerk is involved with one customer; another is working on something else while Vikky, Spiridoula's daughter from Agios Gordis, is processing the rest of us. The idle manager sits chain

162

smoking, occasionally picking up a piece of paper so that he looks busy. He is part of Greece's bureaucratic problem.

There is now no time to pay Proskyr, so it's back to map out where the pool will be. It sounds easy: one metre from the terrace wall and one metre from the future south wall, beside which we will build steps. These will be in line with the sitting room door, so we can still see the sea from inside the house. I plant bamboo poles to mark out the pool's footprint and where Nikos will dig the deep end.

We go off to Proskyr and debate how many cubic metres we have used. "Measure the walls and let me know," Yiannis says. "No problem, come tomorrow." I wonder if this is standard procedure.

We get back and find Valdek is now building little pillars of breeze blocks in the corners and along the sides. Nikos Bulldozer has still not come, so I phone him.

"I'll be an hour," he says.

"Big problem," says Valdek, "the terrace is 45 cm too low. I will get Alexos. We will need 45 cubic metres more of concrete."

I calculate what it will cost; we'll be £800 over budget. Perhaps we must lower the pool and have a step down from the veranda. Or maybe Nikos will dig out enough earth from the deep end to spread in over the shallow end so this also raises the pool.

We can only solve the problem once Nikos Bulldozer has arrived. I phone him again.

"Don't worry," he says. "I'm coming down from Sinarades."

Tension builds. Will Nikos get here before Alexos Hirdaris? The Athenians don't seem to worry; they have their theodolite and it's a hot sunny day and the girls on the beach are topless.

Nikos arrives in his bulldozer, hurtles up our road into the hairpin bend. No crab cornering now: it's the full wheel of death approach. The outside wheels climb the safety wall, the bulldozer leans over and Nikos comes into sight. The Athenians panic in front of the monster JCB. They pick up their bags of cement, their spades and, most important, their theodolyte; then dive for cover. They leave their empty water bottles and plastic bags; they are already picking up bad Greek habits.

The problem seems to fade. "I'll wait for Alexos," says Nikos. "Can I have a coffee?"

Nescafé, sugar, cold water in a 1.5 litre plastic water bottle and shake like crazy. "One English *frappé*, Nikos."

"Bravo, John."

We wait. The Athenians look at the girls on the beach. Nikos drinks his coffee. We discuss the party. "It cannot be in the afternoon," says Nikos. "We should have it at 9.30 in the evening. That's when all parties are in Greece." He grins and adds: "And when we swim."

With his coffee finished, Nikos gets into the JCB. Seven scoops and he digs half the deep end. The scoop digs in, the JCB lifts itself up off its legs and Nikos moves the bulldozer to the side. Another seven scoops and he digs the rest of the deep end. The earth and more old pipes are dumped next to the terrace wall, so reducing the 45 centimetre deficit.

Nikos then tackles the slope up to the shallow end. It is an impressive solo performance of bulldozing under conductor Valdek's waving baton. First, he drags the scoop lower and brings the earth into the deep end. Then he digs this out and heaps it to one side. Finally he repeats the process with the two side slopes.

Alexos has now arrived to discuss the terrace with an altitude problem. "There is no way we can have the pool balanced on 40 cm breeze block columns," he exclaims. "We can have 20 cm columns, and have the pool a single step lower than the veranda."

I am happy. I have finished up with what I had originally planned. It is interesting how Greeks are prepared to negotiate a compromise; though Alexos probably doesn't have much choice.

Alexos calculates that it will take ten hours to build the pool, so the Athenians could be ready by 5.00 tomorrow afternoon to pour the concrete. He phones Yiannis at Proskyr, who tells him that the pump has been booked for 7.00 in the morning. After a shouting match, Alexos agrees to be ready by 3.00. After an invitation to the party, which he accepts with enthusiasm, he is off.

Nikos by now has finished the deep end and drives down the road to pick up the breeze blocks and remaining bags of cement. What would we do without him? As he leaves I remind him that I must pay him. He's very laid back about such matters. Maybe his paperwork is not as good as his excavating.

An order for two *cafés frappés* with milk is placed. The word is getting around that the chef has mastered this act. The younger Christos, the Albanian, is teased that he's a baby as he only drinks milk. In view of his enthusiasm on the theodolite, God help the girls when he grows up.

Serious work now starts. Five 20 cm breeze block pillars are erected under each side of the future pool with three at each end. Adjustments to height to bring them all level are achieved by the great Greek art of recycling. A search party is dispatched to find bricks, broken or whole, and surplus marble floor tiles which are then cemented onto the pillars as needed. One day a Greek builder is going to have a problem: he will arrive at a tidy site.

Nikos has dug a crude deep end with slopes coming down from four sides. Now the team turn to gardening – digging and dragging earth until they have the right shape. Finally the older Christos uses my rake to smooth out the surface. I'm glad that all my tools are being used. What appears to be a primitive method produces a perfectly sculptured hole into which, in six and a half weeks time, engineers and builders will dive.

The sun goes down in a glorious golden hue. I tell them the name of my house: *Iliovasilema*, sunset. They stop work for a moment.

"*Poly oraia!*" Very beautiful.

Work stops again, they need something else; I haven't a clue what they are saying. Then young Christos raises his arms together and brings them down in front of him.

"A pickaxe, of course."

We go in search of one, but only find a classic Mediterranean hacking digger which Pavlos has left. Valdek grabs it and excavates guilty rocks which are sticking through the surface. Then it's back to gardening, smoothing the land.

Nikos Mechanikos phones from his office. He is impressed with progress. He tells me that the final signature on the final piece of paper was made in the morning. It seems the job of the engineer is to fight the bureaucracy. No wonder there are so many empty shells on the island. A few are because people run out of money, but most will be derelict because of the planning process. Either the owner of the land has applied for planning permission and is still waiting or he has gone ahead without a permit and been caught by the police.

As darkness falls and the new moon cuts a useless crescent in the blackening sky, the boys give up. The Poles accept a beer or two and we discuss Panathanaikos, Olympiakos and Manchester United. They've done well today. I think that the immigrants are the ones that can roll up their sleeves and work hard. But this would be unfair on Pavlos and his team. They also work flat out, when they turn up. Farewell from Valdek is "early, early". We'll see them at seven.

Wednesday 25 July, 42 down and 5 to go

It's early in the morning. I need to water the walls before the workers arrive. The question on my mind is will *pastitsada* and dance, plus a few fair northern maidens, have weakened our warriors' energy. At 7.10 the Athenian team turns up. Unlike the Corfiots who shout and debate which plank goes where, these boys work in unison. Maybe Valdek is the boss, but they discuss, agree and get on with the job.

While the two Poles lay out the mesh on the future base of the pool with Valdek cutting it to fit around the sixteen little pillars, Christos, the Albanian, brings up the metal rods. It's not a hierarchical issue. Each will collect and fetch when they are not busy building. With eight hours before the concrete comes, the urgency is impressive. Of the ten hours' work, three were done last night. That leaves only one hour for contingencies.

It is still not 8.00 and the base mesh is in place, the two layers wired together. The team now goes down to bring up the panels. Who wants to play Lego, when you can build a pool out of large plastic pieces? It turns out that Valdek has two children, one of three and the other just two months old. I ask him if he knows Lego, "building with plastic". He grins.

"My daughter makes houses with her Lego, I make *piscines* with mine."

Four-metre steel rods are now brought up and laid around the perimeter of the pool. Valdek, who owns the wire cutter, turner and tightener, works his way round connecting the rods to the mesh. The two Christoses fit nuts and bolts to the telescopic tubes which will be the struts to support the panels. One of the selling points of the pool was that the struts hold up the walls pressing in when the pool is full and pulling out when the pool is empty. This flexibility is vital if there is an earthquake. In contrast, a concrete pool that cracks is finished.

167

After a short coffee break - this time hot not cold - the panels are moved to sit on the pillars. By 9.00, the first one is in place. Alexos phones to check how things are going and tells the boys that the concrete will arrive at 2.00, an hour early. There goes the contingency. It is now "quickly, quickly" not "slowly, slowly."

I phone our daughter Louise to report on progress and parties. Her son, little Peter wants a word.

"Can I dive into the pool?" he asks.

"Yes, it's very deep."

"I'll race you, Pops."

"How many lengths?" I ask.

"Only one," he replies.

"One hundred, you mean," I suggest.

All three grandchildren are good swimmers, but I reckon my stamina is better than their speed. We compromise on twenty.

Louise comes back on. "Can you get solar panels to heat the water? I want it nice and hot in October."

"I'll investigate," I reply. She's happy.

I walk down to the valley to pick up the *Guardian*. "World deal on climate isolates US" is the headline. "With the notable exception of the US - the most powerful and polluting nation - the world has adopted the Kyoto protocol." My solar panels are a small contribution. If they work, I'll put some up in England.

By 11.00, the pool panels are fitting and the struts are in place. Metal rods are dropped vertically into the corrugated bulges and are tied to horizontal rods which lie in a gulley along the top of the panels. These will strengthen the frame and hold the panels together. Valdek measures diagonally across the pool to make sure it forms a rectangle. He then adjusts the telescopic struts until the pool sides are straight.

"Three hours to go, Valdek," I announce.

"No problem. Two *cafés frappés* please," he replies.

They deserve them. Christos, the non-coffee drinking Albanian, carries on bolting the panels together.

"Christos, do you play football?" I ask him when he joins us.

"No, in summer I work and in winter I study Electronics."

Christos the Pole meanwhile gets out the theodolite and checks up on the topless girls on the beach.

"Would you like to look?" he asks. I cannot refuse.

"They're mainly from Sweden, Denmark and Germany," I inform them knowingly.

We could have a problem; work stops as everyone wants to look. I'm amused by Valdek's enthusiasm, as he's the married man.

"It's OK," says Christos the Pole. "He's married to my sister."

"So what are your plans for the future?" I ask them.

"We'll return to Poland when we have saved enough money," says Valdek.

This is a lesson for us in England. The Eastern Europeans will work very hard, pay their taxes and then return to their homeland or maybe settle if they marry a local girl. To them Europe is just a large place to move around and work in. In many ways this fluid existence is similar to that in the US.

Their entertainment is over; Valdek sets up the theodolite near the pool. For an hour the two Poles minutely adjust the pool for height.

With an hour to spare, the Poles sit down for a beer and some lunch, and then lie back for a short siesta. Christos, the Albanian, carries on working, putting rocks outside the pool, so that the concrete can come out about 80cm. He then asks for newspapers.

"Are English papers OK?" I ask.

"It doesn't matter," he replies. I'm impressed.

Instead of reading them, he wraps them around his feet and then climbs into his Wellington boots. I reckon he'll be the concrete paddy man.

Nikos Mechanikos phones. He cannot believe we are ready. I didn't say: "I told you so," but I think he got the message.

Nikos Builder had been to the office and they had agreed what he will do for me. Nikos Mechanikos knows nothing about the quality of his work and proposes to use him for a couple of days on one of his other projects. I don't like the idea.

Nikos Builder has asked for £4,000 as a first payment. I check in my bank pass book and tell Nikos Mechanikos that it won't be too much of a problem. I notice a new line has appeared under the last drachma entry. It's in euros. It looks as if Greece will be ready for the change-over in five month's time. The British Eurosceptics say they won't and everything will be a shambles. Wake up, Britain; the rest of Europe is moving on.

Yiannis, from Proskyr, phones. "Are you ready for the concrete?" he asks.

"Of course," I reply. "We are the Athenian team".

He laughs.

We wait and have a beer or two under the olive tree with the breeze cooling us. The Poles certainly like their beer. Christos, the Albanian, is on Coke.

Eventually the pump arrives and the pouring can begin. It drops a dollop in the bottom of the pool, and then around the outside to form a base through which concrete won't pass from the inside of the pool. Valdek moves to the shallow end and defines the perimeter with a mound of concrete. Christos the Pole pushes and then smoothes the concrete to the edge of the pool with a plank.

Valdek, always in the lead, pours around the deep end. The concrete starts to slide towards the bottom of the pool, where Christos the Albanian is shoving it back. The team is synchronised, pour, push, smooth. They work from out to in, swapping from the shallow end to the deep and back as the concrete dries. They end up in the centre of the deep end.

With the bottom of the pool finished, Valdek climbs onto the top of the panels. He guides the elephant's trunk into corrugated hollows in the back of the panels. When each is full he moves on. The concrete comes out in great spurts so, in a frenzy, he must fill two or three holes at a time. As the next load comes rushing through, the trunk struggles to get free of his grip. The only problem is that stones in the concrete are sprayed both outside and inside the pool so its smooth floor surface begins to look like a lunar landscape.

Nikos Mechanikos arrives. His first words sum everything up. "I can't believe my eyes."

Is it a comment on the plastic pool or the vast amount of work that has been done? In over four weeks we made a 15 metre wall. In the eleven days since he was last here, we have filled the wall and made the road, excavated the top terrace, built 25 metres of wall and constructed a swimming pool. I would like to think he was impressed by my management skills; we have had a programme and we have all worked as a team. Nikos Bulldozer worked the first weekend; Pavlos started at 7.30 in the morning and came in on Saturday, and our Athenians have worked all the daylight hours.

He likes the level of the pool and but he is worried about the north wall.

"To build a terrace between here and the pool will require another supporting wall next to the pool," he insists.

My temperature and blood pressure rises. "Alexos says we don't," I lie. "The Athenians will put long bars into the panels as the concrete sets. These we will turn to the horizontal to help hold up the terrace."

"Then we must fill the void between the pool and the north wall with earth," he says.

"But we can't get the bulldozer to that end any more," I argue. "We could build a pillar in the centre of the terrace to help support it. Alexos says the pool will hold up one side."

"OK then, if there's a problem it's Alexos's fault." Either he is annoyed that Alexos has become the Engineer or, more probably, he still doesn't accept my plastic pool.

"All right then, let's phone Alexos," I say. Alexos confirms that there won't be a problem. Maybe one day I can get Nikos round to liking my pool, but I doubt it.

I tell him about the problem I had in getting the Land Rover around the hairpin bend in our road.

"Change your car," he proposes. "I'm swapping my BMW for a Mercedes and that'll be OK."

"How about cutting the corner of the boxes?" I ask.

"You could weaken them," he counters.

"Then let's widen the bend with a cantilever section on the outside," I suggest.

"Now that's a good idea." As an engineer, he fancies an exciting project. We then move on to discuss Nikos Builder. "I saw him today and we agreed what he would do. But I told him he would have to work for me, so when he was not building your house he would be on one of my projects. Then I'll know where he is." Maybe he's right. My own management abilities have been seriously tested by my failure to control Pavlos's projects.

"But we only have six weeks to my son's arrival and everything must be finished by then," I venture.

"Not if it's the wrong thing."

By now it is 7.30 - twelve hours of non-stop work. The pool team are watering the concrete. Their day is done. I promise to give it another watering in the evening. I think the word is getting around about my expertise.

Moments later, Alexos phones to check that everything is alright. Just as we are off for our evening swim, he arrives with a potential client. I think he's really a salesman not an engineer. The salesman's standard answer is "no problem". The engineer, on the other hand, always says, "there's a problem, let's solve it." He goes down to see his team. I hope it is to tell them what to do tomorrow rather than join them in the fun I am sure they are having.

Thursday 26 July, 43 days down and 4 to go

If Corfiots get to work at 7.30, the Athenians get to work at 7.00. They sweep the pool with my broom and bring over the breeze blocks. In the northeast corner they start to build the Roman Stairs - a fancy name for what all good pools have, steps at the shallow end.

Our own plan for the day is to get away from the house; we savour these days. First stop will be Proskyr, who say they delivered 26 cubic metres, while Pavlos and I say 25. I have to measure the walls - a GCSE Maths challenge. No walls are ever simple but the page of calculations is enough to fool anyone. I arrive at 24.2 which seems to impress Yiannis at Proskyr. He accepts my figure.

Instead of returning to the Ropa Valley and home, we immediately turn right through the olive groves to Temploni to cross the island and visit some new friends. In the space of 500 metres, we pass from industry 2001 to countryside 1960. A flock of sheep makes its way along the road. They nibble at any juicy morsels on the verge, but there is little at this time of year. We slowly follow as the road is far too narrow to overtake. Ahead we see a mound on the road, but it is moving. It's a tortoise.

We get back onto our secret road to the northeast of the island. Roads and traffic in Corfu radiate out from the town – this route is almost peaceful. However, the concrete suppliers are located in the centre of the island, so the ready-mix man and the pump rule the road. The island's refuse from all the wheelie bins also makes for a huge waste disposal site along a side road, marked by the European twelve star circle sign. I'm pleased my taxes are being used to clean up Corfu.

Five minutes later we pass Danilia, an authentic copy of the traditional Corfu village with *platia*, narrow streets and quaint houses, and a large car park at the entrance. It was built in the 80s by two Italians, so that busloads of tourists could sample a real Greek atmosphere, taste real Greek food in tavernas where they can break plates and buy real Greek souvenirs, probably made in China, at real Greek village shops. It closed within five years. The tourists preferred the tavernas on the beach with their setting sun or rising moon.

Our friends – Norman, now 80, and Barbara, a lot younger – have bought a little newly made house on the road to Poulades. With every visit we see more little boxes being built. Retirees from northern Europe are settling in rural Corfu, where the walking is wonderful and life can be lived at the slow rate of the locals. Norman, suffering from breathing difficulties, finds the moist warm climate perfect. As a bit of a DIY expert he has plenty of challenges – he knows what *avrio* means. Barbara has demanded a pool, which they now have, prefabricated and almost the size of ours. With winters in Corfu surprisingly cold, they have brought solar panels from Austria to heat the water. Perhaps this could also be our solution to a cool pool. I must work out where I can fix solar panels, as there is no way they can go on our lovely traditional roof – when we get it, that is.

Next stop is Rob and Agalis's place. They have just driven down from England and in expectation the builders have made a major effort to clear up. We discuss whether the problem is poor management or poor workers. Rob, an immensely tall sculptor, thinks both are at fault. All his architect wants is to have pictures taken of his artistic creation so that he can have them published in an architectural magazine. Looking good on a grand scale is more important than whether it works or not. I don't know if ours will look good, but it is definitely going to work.

Rob then turns to Greek workmen. "They just don't think." To prove his point, he takes me into one of the bedrooms where fitted cupboards and a dressing table have been installed. He points to where an electric wire comes out of a hole in the wood where a mirror will be put. It is neither in the centre nor near the top where there will be an electric light. The only solution was to have a further panel in front. My conclusion is that one has to be on site whenever work is done.

Maybe Nikos Mechanikos is right. If I am not around, he must manage Nikos Builder. My preferred option is for the latter to leave all the detail until we come back in September. I am still not sure that Nikos Mechanikos has enough time to manage.

We go back past Diellas and stock up with more beer for the Poles. Corfu is in the maximum competition phase of private enterprise at the moment. For such a small island, there is an enormous number of supermarket chains. Fruit and vegetable stalls still flourish and each village has one or two corner shops. We haven't reached the stage we find in the UK where three or four large chains dominate the food business. In many ways Corfu has the best of all worlds. Diellas is best for beer and bottled water; Lidl is best for tins of sardines and tuna; Dimitra has a delicatessen, while the market stalls are best for fresh produce and the local bakery is best for bread.

Our next stop is at Profi, the technical supermarket. This German chain has everything for the DIY enthusiast. Jannie is the master in the hooks and screws department. I like the major civil engineering projects. We buy metres of plastic sheeting to cover the beds and furniture for when the roof comes off. We also need another table for the party. I was amused to read that the "in crowd" in England buys wooden garden furniture, and it's just not done to have plastic. I don't think Greece would score highly in this area. Our final purchase is string. I need to lay out the ramp and the veranda.

We go into town to take £5,000 out of the bank, enough to pay Nikos Bulldozer and Nikos Builder. From our early days in Corfu, I have been impressed with this cash society. Cheques are rarely used, they don't have real value.

Everyone takes round great wads of notes. We find Nikos Mechanikos in great spirits. He is a completely different man now; we are legal.

"You are a very lucky. There were no objections. You must have friends, not enemies, in Agios Gordis," he says.

"My only enemy is Spiros next door," I explain, "but he would be the last person to contact the police, as I have my doubts whether his building is legal."

"Arrange a meeting tomorrow afternoon with the two Nikoses and Pavlos," he proposes. "Make it at 5.00 or 6.00 as I have a 7.30 meeting in town. Phone me when you have Pavlos's agreement."

I then explain some of my ideas on the pool terrace and he tells me to draw up detailed plans, so we can get everyone's agreement. Anna's plan had shown 40 cm square pillars to hold up the veranda roof. Pavlos had told me to go for 30 cm ones. Now Nikos Builder wants them to be 24 cm. I like 30 cm as this is the depth of a stair tile. I have suddenly become a trainee architect and engineer. In truth, if I hadn't been a computer engineer, I would have liked to have built houses. I have inherited some of my builder father's Irish blood.

Details must include exact measurements. What could be seen as a minor issue, the height of the wall between the veranda and the pool is now highly significant. It must be low enough for us to sit on and high enough to stop our fifteen-month-old grandson, Sean, from climbing over. He had held the world record for the twenty metre dash for eight-month-olds. When he comes in September, he'll probably be into high hurdling.

When we get home I phone Des, our daughter-in-law, to explain my dilemma. "I'm worried about Sean. You've told me he can climb anything. If my wall is less than his waist height, he'll be able to get his upper body on the wall and, as he's top heavy, will be able to bring up his legs and over he'll go into the pool. Tell me, how far his chest is from the ground?" I ask

Des, the fashion designer, has a tape measure ready and comes back moments later. "Twenty-two inches."

"But he was thirteen months old yesterday. He's tall."

"No, he's huge," she says.

I then phone Pavlos and tell him the pool is finished. Can he come next day at 5.00? With lots of *yia sou*, the informal "health to you", he agrees.

The pool team, meanwhile, has built the Roman Stairs and is now laying a screed over the steps and the pool bottom. This involves Christos the Albanian mixing cement and sand on the terrace with my spade and the two Poles slapping it on and then smoothing it. They have found by the house a large saucepan in which we boil water when we have a power cut. This is now being used to carry the mixture; I wondered what they will use next.

The Poles then move into the depth of the pool, where it is like a furnace. With the temperature outside in the mid 30s, the black walls are acting like a solar heating system. As fast as they apply the cement it dries, so they work at a frantic pace. Cries of "beer" come out of the "black hole of Corfu". I satisfy the Poles' thirst for twenty minutes or so and then I hear the cries again. As the day goes on we have two plastered plasterers on our hands.

To show solidarity with the workers, I construct a pillar from unused breeze blocks in the centre of the void to the north of the pool. It is here that I want Pavlos to build the support for the pool terrace.

Alexos is due to arrive at 7.30 so the team has worked for twelve hours non-stop through the heat of the day, except for short breaks to look through the theodolite at the beach below. He phones and says he will be half an hour late. He asks me to take Christos, the Albanian, down to Spiridoula before 8.00 as he has paid till then, and give her the balance due. If the team could use our outside shower, I could deduct £4 from the bill as they wouldn't need Spiridoula's. He would pay me later.

Christos has enough money, so he pays the full amount and we return with their luggage. Alexos arrives soon after and is pleased with the work, but he is very unhappy about the £4 – a rather sad attitude to take.

As the team shower and change, I show Alexos the supporting pillar. He confirms that the steel rods sticking up from the corrugations in the pool wall will be bent horizontal to be the base for the pool terrace and will not damage the pool. He's happy and so am I. Nikos Mechanikos won't get his supporting wall beside the pool.

Alexos agrees that a team will arrive on Monday 3 September, two days before we return to Corfu. They will paint the plastic walls white, instal the liner and fix the Filterblock over the edge of the deep end. We calculate to the nearest centimetre how much space Pavlos must leave in the pool terrace for the pump. I now begin to worry that I am not here during the work. We debate where the rails for the pool cover will go. There seems to be a lot of details to sort out.

We stand beside the pool admiring its position. With no surround to the pool on the sea side, the surface of the water will merge with the sea and the horizon. We return to why engineers don't like plastic pools.

"They don't get so much money building them," he says.

"How's that?" I ask.

"Engineers in Greece get a commission on the steel you use and the concrete you pour."

I think about Nikos Mechanikos. If this was the case he should be encouraging me to pour more concrete, yet he had saved me £10,000 by not having Zacharias's original retaining wall for the road. I conclude that Greeks can talk very badly about other Greeks. I wonder what they say about the foreigners.

By now, it's time to say goodbye. Jannie comes out and they ask her to look through the theodolite. I think she'll be asking for one for her birthday, not to look at the boys on the beach but the birds in the trees.

178

"It's better than my binoculars," she hints.

It's sad to see them go; they have been good company, particularly Christos the Albanian. He had told me about the valley in the mountains where he had come from. I tell him that it must have been along this valley that the Italians came when they attacked Greece in 1941. It would be fun to visit it with a local, but we didn't have time to arrange it.

The team leaves with Alexos. The Poles will go by ferry to Patras and on by bus to Athens. Alexos cannot get a cabin, so they will sleep on deck. Christos will stay the night in Corfu and drive the truck back via Igoumenitsa in the morning. We have been teasing him that he will be staying on with one of the beautiful girls he has seen on the beach. He has fallen in love with Corfu. I tell him he will always be welcome for a swim and a Coke.

My view of the 2004 Olympics is now more positive. In 2 days and 3 hours, the three Athenians have done a fantastic job. Admittedly they are not Greeks, but it will be the energy of the East Europeans that will build the Parthenon of the 21st century.

We then plan where the boughs will fall: not on the house, nor in the pool and, most definitely not on Spiros's apartments.

Motivating Pavlos

Friday 27 July, 44 down and 3 to go

Today everyone will meet here to plan the final phase. I am still worried about Pavlos. The last ten days have been fantastic: he has delivered on the work he promised. But he and Nikos Mechanikos don't talk to each other. When we leave on Monday, will Pavlos get up to his old tricks? He now has the key role to play, building a terrace round the pool, so that we can lay tiles and then complete the pool.

My real question is how to motivate him. The Greeks would shout at him. This I cannot do as he doesn't understand me and I won't be here anyway. I could get Nikos to do the shouting, but that hasn't worked before; and Nikos will also be away for two weeks at the critical point. We could threaten him that we'll give the work to someone else. This a great idea in theory but only Nikos can organise it and he's got too much work already. Alternatively I could offer him a bonus on completing the work. I sense Pavlos is not primarily motivated by money. I would like to think that part of the reason why he's worked well recently, is that he is now happier with his English boss than at the start, when he probably thought I was an idiot, which I was. I decide that I must give him a "Henry V before Agincourt" speech.

Nikos Mechanikos arrives at 4.30 absolutely knackered; he had been going non-stop since the early hours of the morning. "Bread, olives, oil and some cold water, Jannie," he orders and sits down under the olive tree to cool off. He looks over to the pool and says a few nice words. He checks out my plans and approves them.

"Where does the water go?" he asks.

I refrain from saying "In the pool" and reply, "You are the engineer."

"We need a groove along the outside of the veranda wall so the water runs away."

He was talking about the torrential rain Corfu has in the autumn and winter and the overflow from the pool made by the grandchildren when they get over enthusiastic.

"But we can't insert a groove as the pool is exactly four tiles from the wall."

"So we'll have some holes in the tiles," he proposes.

I look surprised.

"Don't worry, water goes everywhere in Greece." We then move on to the pool terrace, between the pool and the north wall. "They are the same height," says Nikos.

"I know, they used a theodolite," I reply flippantly.

"The water won't run off the terrace. Don't worry, we'll knock some holes in the north wall, so the water can drain away."

"I like that; it'll run into the jardinière, an automatic watering system."

Finally we move round to where the ramp will be built. "It's too narrow," he starts, "and these struts will get in the way."

"But the slope will cover the struts," I argue.

"Not this one at the bottom of the slope." He gives it a kick and it moves. He gives it another kick and it wobbles. "We'll throw it away," he concludes.

I lose my temper. "You bloody well won't as you'll be throwing away any guarantee from Piscines Ideales if the side caves in."

"Bah, they won't pay anything if this load of rubbish collapses. You can have a ramp or you can keep the strut; you can't have both," he insists.

"Yes, we can," I reply.

"How?"

"Because I say so."

Maybe he is winding me up. He certainly succeeds.

At that point, Nikos Bulldozer turns up. He sits down under the olive tree and orders a glass of water. He lacks his normal urgency; it dawns on me it's payment time. I ask him how much I owe him and he produces a scrap of paper on which seven figures had been written, giving a total of £1,000. I had expected a figure of £800 but I had forgotten the four full lorry loads of hardcore. At not much over £1 per tonne, I am more than happy. I pay him the cash and he signs my receipt book. I give him his copy and he returns it. "Take it to England," he says.

"Our bulldozer hero doesn't like paper work. He's just an action man," volunteers Nikos Mechanikos.

The two Nikoses now discuss the work to be done. The excavation for the south wall foundation won't be a problem. The land he digs up will fill the ramp. Again he says no problem. This is why I like him – he has no problems. We turn to Nikos Mechanikos's brilliant idea: we can excavate the olive tree terrace, where we are now sitting, and build an underground garage so the car won't spoil the view. Nikos Bulldozer relishes another attack on the mountain and points to the historic rock on which, thirty years before, we had toasted the future.

"I want to dig it up so access to the garage will be simpler," says Nikos Bulldozer.

"But John has taken four weeks exposing it," says Nikos Mechanikos with a big grin.

"Tomorrow one of England's greatest sculptors is coming and he'll decide," I say, referring to Rob, Elena's son-in-law.

They accept that, in this case, art is more important than engineering.

With business complete we go back to sit under the olive tree and wait for one of the builders. There is a roar from below and the third Nikos arrives in a cloud of dust. He will win the gold medal if they have moped hill-climbing at the Olympics.

"Phone Pavlos, John," says Nikos Mechanikos. "You told everyone I have a meeting in town at 7.30. That means I leave in half an hour. He's always late."

"He's probably asleep," suggests Nikos Builder.

I phone and wake him up.

"Has Nikos arrived?" asks Pavlos.

"He's been here an hour and half and he goes in thirty minutes," I reply.

"I'll be there in twenty minutes, don't worry."

I could see my motivational speech is necessary. I return to find the three Nikoses discussing the party. Nikos Bulldozer says again that it's always better to have a party in the evening. He's obviously very busy in the day, even if it will be on a Sunday.

Nikos Builder has his arms outstretched. "We'll cook a fish - this big."

Not to be outdone, Nikos Mechanikos says, "I'll bring 50 litres of my wine."

"It's going to be some party," I say but then add: "But only if everything is finished."

Nikos Bulldozer leaves and the other two discuss the schedule of work that must be done when I am away: drains to be laid and connected to the soakaway, the veranda and a new roof for the house, a 55 cm safety wall around the periphery of the pool area and, finally, electrical services for the pool. A start could also be made on the structure for the extension. Nikos Builder is happy with this and he is obviously going to get it ready for 9 September as he is keen on the party as well. He likes my drawings: they even show where the cables and pipes go. He sees no problems.

I like our new builder. He has arrived at the house at odd hours just to check how things are going. His huge grin is always turned on. I pay him his £4,000 down payment and his grin gets bigger.

"But you only get the £8,000 when all the work is finished," I tell him.

His grin is now splitting his face. "And we have a party," he adds. He then goes.

Another happy man then turns up – at last. Pavlos is looking extremely smart in white shirt and ironed trousers. This a different person to the wall builder with concrete splattered all over. I give him a copy of the plans.

"Very beautiful, John," he says and puts them in his pocket. "Now Nikos, let's look at the work I have to do."

He raises sensible objections. I could see that he needs time to digest what he has to do, but Nikos Mechanikos doesn't have the time, and tries to say goodbye. Then Pavlos has other questions. I sense they don't love each other. Eventually Nikos leaves without the list of telephone numbers I had prepared for him.

I am now left with Pavlos. I ask him to come up to sit under the olive tree, where my notebook lies. I find the great speech I have made, written out in Greek. He looks over and reads it even quicker than I can say it.

"For a thousand years, my family have been soldiers," I have written, referring to the ancestor who came over with William the Conqueror. "In 1641, we fought in Ireland where we stayed. My father fought in the first world war in Palestine against the Turks." I thought this would go down well with a Greek. "Now *my* battle is to complete the pool. I hope together we will win."

At this point, he's finished reading and puts out hand and says, "OK, John. I do my work."

"My family motto is 'honour and truth', Pavlos." We shake again but I am not sure if he sees this as applying to himself. But I have a final point which I know will clinch the deal. I have looked up a quote from Herodotus, who claimed that the Persian general had said before going into battle with the Greeks: "Alas, Mardonius, what kind of people have you brought us to fight against? They do not compete for money but for pride!"

He smiles. The message has got through. He then leaves. I wonder if I should have suggested that finishing the pool is, to me, like completing the Olympics on time.

Saturday 28 July, 45 days down and 2 to go

Alternate Saturdays are Fred's days. Today we have to cut down two huge poplars. The bigger one is right next to where the extension would be built and will dump its leaves into the pool in the autumn. The other is near the hairpin bend of our new road and blocks our view.

It is one of those days when everything goes wrong. We put the fully extended ladder up against the big tree. My job is to climb up to the top, and then throw a rope over the end of each of the five huge boughs. I will pass it through a loop at one end and then tighten it, so I can pull at the appropriate moment once Fred has made the necessary cut. At first I cannot throw the rope out far enough. Then I attach it to a six metre bamboo, which becomes a javelin. Hurling a javelin when perched on top of the ladder is bad enough, but it just wants to get stuck in the branches. Fred urges me on from below.

"Don't fall off," he calls.

I'm glad that no Greeks are watching. Since childhood they have been scaling olive trees and have lost all fear of heights. Now they would climb out to the end of each bough and tie the rope on there.

We then plan where the boughs will fall: not on the house, nor in the pool and, most definitely not on Spiros's apartments. After great debate, I hand over to Fred. Unfortunately, his chain saw is playing up. I am surprised he hasn't asked for a new one considering the number of trees we have cut down. He comes down the ladder to fix it. He then goes up again. So it goes on. At last the saw is biting and he stops.

"Shit, the saw has got stuck," he announces. Then he says, with brutal honesty, "It's *my* fault."

He struggles to free the blade. Eventually he's ready. He races down the ladder and together we pull. Nothing budges. So up the ladder he goes. After repeating this a few times, the bough comes crashing down and we both fall down the mountain causing minor injury and some embarrassment.

Today is not Fred's day. Of five boughs, two crash into the pool and one on to Spiros's place. One goes uphill instead of down. The last one is perfect.

Finally the main trunk falls and fits exactly into where the pool terrace will be. At least, the pool stands up well to the battering. We now have to saw up the boughs and move the wood over to Spiros's boundary. The pile of branches grows higher and creates a barrier between ourselves and our neighbour. As fires are forbidden in Greece in the summer, it will stay there for three months.

Spiros's woman watches the action.

"Good day, Stella," I say.

She points to the wood. "We will have snakes," she says.

I ignore her negative attitude. I don't even point out that her cats will kill the snakes.

"It's best to ignore your Greek neighbours," Fred suggests. I think he's right as far as Spiros is concerned.

Four hours and four beers later, Fred's time is up. He tells me it's the worst job he's done this year. I think he looks forward to my departure. He has two more Saturdays, before I return, to cut the logs into size and prune our beloved olive tree.

Saturday is serious siesta time. However I have to get up to remove all the small branches, twigs and leaves from the pool. Elena, Rob, Agalis and their son, Marco, are due at 7.00. I now realise the hell the Athenians had worked in. The pool is like an oven. Eventually, all evidence of the tree is removed, and no damage has been done.

Our visitors arrive by our own road, a pretentious word for a track up the mountain. They come up on to the upper terrace and see a building site ahead with the ugly black plastic ribbed wall of the pool jutting out from the house. With stairs and ramp still to be made, we offer them a ladder to climb to get up to the olive tree terrace.

Rob leads with Marco. Agalis and Elena, who is limping badly, follow.

"The fact that Elena has come up shows she likes you, John," says Rob. "She was stung on her foot by a bee, just before we left home."

They are all enthusiastic about the pool. In a few years time, when their house is complete, they will probably get one themselves. The fact that its construction is trouble-free appeals to Rob as they have been building for five years and they still haven't finished.

Rob is in his element. "This takes me back to my construction site; it's always exciting when one is starting."

I had to admit that I had been excited over the last six weeks, as well as depressed and furious and, above all, frustrated.

We return down the ladder to look at my stone, which Nikos Bulldozer wants to destroy. It is rectangular in shape, two metres high, one metre wide and 60 centimetres thick. Lying at an angle of 45%, it is of historic interest (as Elena also remembers standing on it thirty years ago) rather than of artistic merit.

"You have three options. You can stand it up and have a menhir," suggests Rob. "You can leave it as it is as a feature to be seen by people turning the corner, or you could move it and lay it down as a bench. I am a great believer in sculpture that can be used. Maybe you could carve a pattern on the top, something geometric, perhaps."

We vote for the third solution, which will please Nikos Bulldozer who can move it, satisfy me as I want to keep it and interest Jannie as it could be a focus in her garden. There is an obvious place to put it, on the southernmost box, on the inside of our hairpin bend and in line with the view of the beach below and Ortholithi in the distance.

Sitting on the rock, one would have a view not only of the sea but also of the sunset even in midsummer, when it is usually blocked by Spiros. Looking back towards the house we would see our '*bodzo*', the pool walls which will be clad with stone, with bougainvillea and honeysuckle climbing above the garage.

It is now Agalis's turn to contribute. She points to huge straggling bushes behind the stone. "What will you do with the myrtle when the stone is moved?"

To most people myrtle is a scruffy shrub growing wild everywhere on the island. To Agalis, the artist and potter with a fine Greek face and a deep affection for nature inherited from her parents, it has remarkable properties.

"First, it brings you good luck," she says. "Secondly, in the warm still evenings, it exudes a delicious smell. Thirdly, and of greatest importance, it is an excellent deterrent of insects."

So now I knew why people, staying at Michael below and Spiros next door, complain so bitterly about the mosquitoes, while we have so few. In fact sitting under the olive tree, we are rarely ever bitten. Jannie is a long-term member of the pro-myrtle camp; she thinks the white feather-like flowers that appear in June are gorgeous.

Fred has cut back a large myrtle bush behind the house and it is now producing new shoots right back to the roots. Maybe he could transfer the bushes and plant them around our rock seat right up to the concrete corner of the box. It would act as a hedge hiding the concrete and give us protection against our flying foes in the evening.

189

At this point Elena, who is pro-myrtle and likes the stone, asks the obvious question.

"Why do you need to remove the stone in the first place?"

"So we can bring the car right up and park it out of sight in a garage under the olive tree terrace," I reply.

"Why not leave the car on the corner below the boxes," she suggests. "You won't be able to see it from the house and you won't endanger your wonderful olive tree." She thinks for a moment and then plays her ace. "And John, you will save money."

She knows me too well and we all agree that Nikos Meckanikos's great idea should be rejected.

With our work done, we drive down to the beach and walk to Theodoros. We swim as the sun is going down. The waves are long and strong as they roar over the sand bank. Rob, without his board, body-surfs in, riding on the largest waves, stands up laughing and struggles out again. Where on earth could there be such a paradise?

We all eat fish, cooked to perfection by Maria, drink Fotis's delicious white wine, a Greek Pinot Grigio, and discuss building with Tassos, who always checks the length of the stubble on my chin to find out how the pool project is progressing. I am clean shaven.

With the sun gone, the sky turns from red to purple to black. The foam of the waves is a brilliant white in the darkness. Now all his guests have left, Fotis sits alone looking out to sea, to a sea which is silver in the half moon which is now above Ortholithi. His philosophy of enjoying nature and rejecting Mammon has much to offer.

Six happy Corfiots walk back along the beach, sand underfoot and stars above. We say goodbye.

Sunday 29 July, 46 days down and 1 to go

Throughout the day we clear the land of builders' rubbish and the house of the dust made since we arrived. In some ways, it's a pointless exercise as we know that when we return everywhere will be far more of a mess than it is now.

For our last night, with the car loaded for an early departure next morning, we go down to the beach to say goodbye to our other friends, Michael and Anna. Running the Romantic View below as well as the Romantic Palace on the beach has imposed a strain on them both; and they are still only halfway through the season. We order his speciality, numerous Greek meze with a couple of mayonnaise-based salads, all served on a huge plate in the style of an Italian *antipasto*. In size and in content it goes down well with his German clients as a starter. For us it is a meal in itself. He brings us a half-litre of his red wine, home made in Kato Pavliana, a village on the south slopes of the mountain of Garouna. Jannie claims it is more mellow that any other on the island.

"I will check all is OK, when you are away," he offers.

"Thank you, dear Michael, you have been a support throughout the summer, even it was just to cheer me up," I tell him. "But you already have too much on your plate."

He sits down and replies: "We are lucky, the children are now doing all the waiting." He pauses and then continues. "With the new and the old buildings above and the taverna and rooms here, we have three places; one for each of them if they want to stay on when they grow up."

I think how typically Greek he is – building for the future of his family. As if to prove that he can relax for a few moments, he stays and talks about my plans. I am more interested in his past. Michael tells us his story.

"I was the younger son in the family. I went to Berlin as a sixteen year old. The poverty to the east of the Wall shocked me; the prosperity in the west excited me. Through hard work and a lot of luck, I took the skills I had picked up in my father's taverna in Corfu, through dish-washing, pizza-making and waiting, until I was working in the top Greek restaurant in Germany," he says proudly.

"At twenty-one, I opened my own place, but I missed Corfu so much that I sold up in Berlin and returned to start a taverna on the beach in Agios Gordis. Almost straightaway my father died. Shaken, I went back to Germany and started a lobster and champagne bar in Stuttgart. There I met Anna, fell in love and there is the result," he adds pointing to the three children, each chatting up a customer in Greek, German or English.

I sense that he is building places for his children so that history will not be repeated: in his old age, some of his children will be around him. The ties of the family are still so much stronger in Greece than in Northern Europe. Before we leave, I go into the kitchen to say goodbye to Anna. I admire her immensely.

Monday 30 July, 47 days down and we go

It's a still black starlit night when we get up to catch the ferry. I have forgotten to mark out the step from the veranda terrace to the pool terrace. Jannie's torch has broken overnight, so my metre-wide step may turn out to be something different, perhaps nothing at all.

The ferry to Venice calls first at Igoumenitsa on the mainland. I leave the boat and phone Nikos Bulldozer but there's no answer. That's odd. By 9.00, I would expect him to be at the house.

I phone Nikos Mechanikos who is already at the office. I ask him to phone Pavlos to tell him I have marked on the terrace where I want the stairs, the steps, columns and new wall to go.

Nikos phones Pavlos. He gets the wrong number, so I give him the correct number and he phones again. This time he gets Pavlos and tells me.

"He's playing games again. He's not working at your house. He says it's only a small job. So I tell him I'm not John Waller, I'm Nikos Papavlassopoulos. If he doesn't want the work, I'll put my own men on the job. He says he'll start at 7.30 tomorrow."

Somehow the "tomorrow" doesn't surprise me. Maybe Nikos had been right. We shouldn't be leaving now. Deep down, I believe all will be well as our young engineer may be infuriating with his concrete pool, but my dear old friend Petros Kardakis would never have introduced him to me unless he was confident that Nikos could deliver the work. In nearly seven weeks I had grown to like Nikos. If we do finish on time, I'll be his friend for life.

Meanwhile Nikos Bulldozer has returned with the second tanker load. Water pours out again. We watch it slowly rise and at the critical moment it flows over the skimmer in the filtration unit. George turns on the motor. It works. The two Nikoses and I cheer.

"Now you have a swim, John," orders Nikos Builder.

PART THREE - COMPLETION

Sprinting to the finish

Tuesday 4 September, 2001

The ferry from Venice arrives at 11 at night. The moon – two nights after full – is over Albania and the Greek mainland and lighting up the countryside to Sinarades. Our side of the mountain is still pitch black when we stop on the main road below. Soon we will concrete our own road up but now we climb up the fifty-five remaining steps lit by Spiros's next door. Above the *sterna*, the huge rainwater storage tank, looms a new building, the shell of our extension. The path round the back of the house to the yard where we have the front door is covered in builders' rubble under foot and planks at knee height. Ouch!

We enter and go into the living room, deep in dust, look up and see a gorgeous new wooden roof. Nikos Builder has delivered on his first promise. We go through the French door to what was a small open terrace, to be met not by the twinkle of stars above and the glare of Spiros's lights to the right but by total darkness. The three metre wide veranda on the plan was large. In real life it is immense. No longer can we see our neighbour as the end of the veranda is blocked by the extension.

Ahead of us we see the black plastic pool, just as we had left it in July. Now, to the right, there is a three metre wide terrace next to which we will build our pergola. Between veranda and pool, a metre wide path has been built which extends round to the left of the pool. On the far side, the pool seems to merge with the dark sea below. It is here that we will build the ramp.

Straight ahead of us, to the left of the pool, are the seven steps to the lower terrace where Jannie would like a garden, but could instead provide a turning circle for the car if we want access right up to the house. Now it is just a pile of earth from the excavations, well mixed with more builders' rubble.

"We have just four full days to clear this mess up before Peter and Des arrive," says Jannie. "Let's get to bed."

Wednesday 5 September, 4 full days to go

I wake at 4.00 to a light outside. "That's odd," I think. "It was dark when I went to bed."

I stumble out to find the bright moon above. Now I can see what has been built. Jannie joins me as we inspect our dream.

"My goodness, it is so very beautiful," she says. "Nikos Mechanikos was right."

"We used to have a little summer house. Now we have a hacienda. Look at the veranda roof. Do you remember the plans?" The plans showed it would be almost flat and start below the old eaves, but Nikos Builder had extended the old roof with a subtle curve to connect it to the veranda roof.

"It's lovely," says Jannie.

We move to the far edge of the pool terrace, now nearly a metre and a half above the old boxes, and look back to the house. I put my arms around her. "Do you think it is possible to be romantic about a roof?" I ask, and then, I answer my own question. "I think we can with ours. Her shape is gorgeous and the mottled mix of old and new tiles is so pretty."

We look over the edge. Below us, the moon lights up our olive grove. Perched on our platform, we are now higher than the top of the trees. I look back again at the roof, suspended in the shining moonlight above the dark shadow of the

196

veranda and the house beyond. The view triggers off a memory. Where have I seen this before? The answer suddenly comes.

"Do you remember Jørn Utzon wrote of the Mayan civilisation building a platform above the flat, never-ending rain forest from which they found a completely new dimension on the world. That's what we have now. We can see south with an uninterrupted view to Garouna. And do you remember what inspired Utzon in his design of the Opera House? He visualised buildings constructed not of walls but of roofs. He started with sketches of the curved roof of a pagoda floating above his platform. That is exactly what we have here. Our roof is the same shape as the pagoda's and it really does float above the darkness below."

"I can see what you are saying," replies Jannie, "but we cannot spend the night drooling over a roof. We have work to do in the morning."

There is an odd feeling in the air. Greek nights are normally still. Now the leaves on the poplar are talking noisily to each other and the clouds above are scurrying across the moon.

"They are coming from the south," I say. "That's a warning of bad weather."

We go to bed again, but I am woken an hour or two later by what sounds like Jannie snoring – but she never snores. I hear a gentle murmur then peace. Minutes later there is another murmur. Suddenly there is an odd light – not the light of a car on the road below followed by another light from the road above – but a sort of flash. I then realise that the snoring is distant thunder and the flash is lightning.

At half past seven, the rain starts. The noise is horrendous. The roof of the extension next to our bedroom has not been finished so the wooden ceiling acts as a drum skin. We then notice the water, first as a drip, then as a dribble and finally as a shower. The roof above the bed has not yet been tiled either. So we get up. A storm over the sea is always a sight. We stand on our veranda as the raindrops turn to buckets – but we are dry. The veranda is working.

Ahead, from below the corner of the boxes, I see something move. Up the road, round the corner come two running figures, drenched by the downpour. They are Nikos Builder and his mate; they are here to cover the cement bags. As Kostas runs round with sheets of plastic, Nikos asks us for our comments. We don't tell him about the unfinished roof.

"Nikos, everything is wonderful," I say.

"I am happy that you are happy," he answers.

The sun could have been shining. His large mouth is stretched into an enormous grin. His huge eyes are laughing. From head to toe he is dripping, so he tears off his T-shirt and wrings it out. "We'll be back in a couple of hours when the storm has passed," he promises.

It is time to review progress. The good news is the veranda roof. I check my head doesn't hit the beam which supports it. I have an inch to spare. Six-footers will be alright but taller guests will have to duck.

The bad news is that neither the veranda nor the surrounds of the pool have been tiled. But Nikos Mechanikos has got his own man to cover the area for tiling with a smooth sand-and-cement screed. Our first trip will be to sort out the tiles.

Our next concern is the security of our fourteen-month-old Exocet missile of a grandson. We must erect walls, railings and gates to keep him first on the veranda and secondly, if we can get the pool working, on the terrace which surrounds it.

Of equal concern is the building site we are inviting Peter and Des to. Skips haven't been introduced into Greece, so rubble and rubbish is strewn around, both outside and inside the house. In fairness, the wood of the old roof has mainly been stacked on the moon terrace. The gutters and drainpipes, however, have found their way onto our neighbour's land.

The olive tree terrace and the area behind the house have been used for mixing concrete, which has solidified between piles of sand and stone. The 'no-go' areas will be bigger than the 'go' areas. Below the olive tree terrace is a six foot mound of excavations, roof tiles, wood cut-offs and plastic: water bottles, coffee cups, bags and packing material. This must be cleared.

While we wait for Nikos to return, the big sweep starts. We clear the rubble from the main bedroom – part of the wall has been knocked down to make way for the door into the new bathroom. As we move through the house to remove the remnants of the old roof – torn mouldy black asphalt, birds' nests and rats' homes – a dust storm follows. The bunk room is added to the 'no-go' areas.

Nikos comes back after the rain has gone and we set priorities for the next four days. First we need the safety features. We must be able to trap Sean on the veranda by building a wall around it. Three one metre gaps will be left for access to the pool terrace, the steps and the olive tree terrace. These will need the gates we ordered in July. Our second line of defence will be around the pool terrace. A wall must be built on the north side as part of one of Jannie's jardinières. Somehow we must erect temporary railings along the west side, above the four metre drop into the olive grove below the boxes, and in the south west corner, where there is a deep cavern where we will make the ramp.

Roofing is our second priority. As Peter and Des live in the tropics, they may tolerate a drip of water falling on the bed, but not a deluge. Nikos will have to extend the roof until it covers the extension.

Finally there is the issue of sewage. He has laid the pipe from the house, across and then along the veranda, but it doesn't connect up to the soakaway, which we have lost under the rocks, stones and earth of the new road. I can see this being a problem. Though Jannie and I used the chemical toilet throughout the summer, I think Des will be unhappy. In the Central Highlands of Jamaica, where she comes from, at least they have the jungle in an emergency. I am not sure if our neighbour's olive grove will suffice.

With our builder hard at work, we leave to sort out gates, mattresses and tiles.

Our first task is to get the veranda gates. Mr. Zappas at Grammi is as charming as ever.

"Could you install the gates tomorrow?" I ask.

"Mr. Waller, I'm very sorry. We haven't received them yet."

"But I ordered them three months ago."

Only then do we realise that the order hasn't been passed through to Athens. I go into tantrum mode.

"I will get you temporary gates by Friday," promises Mr. Zappas.

On our way home, we decide to go via Imperial Strom, Corfu's own mattress manufacturer. At least, from previous experience, if they haven't built the two we ordered in July, they will do so in the three days left before Peter, Des and Sean arrive. But – wonder of wonders – there is our order ready for collection. We have lost the gates but won the mattresses – all square and one to play. Now we must sort out the tiles for the veranda and around the pool.

We go off to see Moskou to find out if our tiles have arrived. Sasha is there, all smiles as usual.

"Have you got the tiles I ordered in July?"

"No, you didn't remind me in August. Anyway the manufacturer in Thessaloniki has been on holiday. I can get them by Monday."

The euphoria of the beautiful roof has gone. We are back to the same problems we had with Pavlos. Thoroughly depressed, we return to the house to find Nikos Builder and his mate, Kostas, hard at work building the veranda wall. As fast as Kostas mixes the cement, Nikos lays the bricks for a double wall with an eight centimetre cavity in which he says Jannie should plant flowers. I explain that we will put *skalopatia*, step tiles, with their curved front edges on top to sit on.

As a reward for their efforts I offer them coffee. Nikos has black with one sugar, Kostas has white with much sugar. It turns out he's from Albania.

"From Agii Saranda?" I ask.

"No, from Qyteti Stalin, near Berat."

I'm impressed with the Stalin bit. We find it on my map. He is not from the Greek speaking south of the country but the middle. I deliver Nikos's coffee in a blue mug as blue is the national colour of Greece. Kostas's comes in a red mug.

"For Enver Hoxha," I explain. Nikos thinks this is hilarious; Kostas doesn't.

Work continues at a frantic pace – cleaning inside the house and wall building outside. I check with Alexos Hirdaris what time his pool men would arrive. Originally they were coming the previous Saturday, then Monday and now today. This becomes tomorrow morning – leaving three days to complete a week's work. I have total confidence in them, particularly as Alexos decides the job can be done in two days.

I therefore start phoning round inviting people to the party. Alexos cannot come. Nikos Builder may be alone but could bring a girl or two. Nikos Bulldozer will come and may bring someone. Nikos Mechanikos and Anna are definitely on, so I am left with Pavlos and George. I call my wall builder.

"Pavlos, are you coming to the party?" I ask.

"Yes, John."

"Can you bring your daughter? I speak little Greek, you speak no English, but Maria speaks both."

"OK, John."

"How many will you bring?" I ask.

"How many *can* I bring?" he counters.

"There's you and your wife, George and his wife and Maria. That's five."

"And maybe Maria's boyfriend," he adds.

"That's six – make it seven if you want. Please could you ask Maria to organise your party?" I conclude.

Our final problem is the access road – its surface has disappeared. The top has been washed away in the storm, leaving innocent-looking mud holes between rocks. We could see our guests being stranded on the main road below.

Nikos Mechanikos comes out in the afternoon to show off his creation. He is less stressed out after his holiday. He doesn't threaten to shoot me. In fact, he has done a fantastic job in getting this far. It is always said that no work is done in Greece when one is away. With us, this has not been the case. In fact, we now have most of a new roof, a veranda and a platform around the pool with access by stairs, even if not by ramp. To get Pavlos to deliver was a miracle. Whether it was my battle speech, the idea of a party or Nikos's prompt payment when he finished, nobody will know.

Discussion centres on holes to let water off the pool surrounds. Some have been put between the veranda and the pool but have been covered over when the surface was prepared for tiling. I must crawl under the void below the terrace and find where the holes are, then knock them through to the surface. It sounds easy but it isn't and confirms my theory about wall builders – that they should be small. I barely fit between the pool and the veranda wall. Crawling across rubble, avoiding steel rods sticking out from the wall and struts from the pool, all in the darkness, makes me vow never to go pot-holing. Hard as I look, I cannot find any holes; so it looks as if we will have a five metre wide pool rather than a four metre one.

Thursday 6 September, 3 full days to go

I wake early and, with shorts and T-shirt on, I sweep the veranda. Fory-five square metres of rubbish is removed. I move onto the pool surrounds and the same area is cleared. Soon after 8.00, Nikos Builder and Kostas arrive. I explain to Nikos that I cannot find any holes in the pool surrounds.

"How many do you want?" he asks.

"Four next to the veranda and three at the jardinière end of the pool terrace," I reply.

"No problem," he adds. He then proceeds to knock four holes in the concrete. In fact he had fitted water bottles in position when the concrete had been poured. Having built the fifteen metre veranda wall yesterday, he says today he'll get on with the roof and tomorrow build the six metre north wall, leaving my three drainage holes in the bottom.

A few minutes later Alexos arrives with his two Athenians: George, in his mid forties with a Mexican moustache, and Pavlos, his sidekick in his early twenties. He turns out to be another Albanian. I hope their names were just a coincidence as the other Pavlos and George, the wall builders, had been my big problem

After providing four mugs of coffee, the management leaves the two Athenians to pump rainwater out of the pool. Nikos Builder shows us a small recess in the wall of the new bedroom and a hole in the floor. He'll fix the control panel in the former and feed the electric cables through the latter. We then inspect the hole in the southern end of the pool surrounds where the skimmer, filter and pump will be put. Remarkably it turns out to be the right size. Obviously Pavlos did read my detailed plans.

George, the chief pool man, turns to Alexos. "Where is the *stoko*?"

"John, can you go and get twenty kilos?" asks Alexos.

I can see my role of coffee maker has been extended; I'm now the delivery man as well. Sasha at Moskou has plenty of *stoko*. It turns out to be 'Powder Spatula Material' – used normally for laying tiles. On our return, the pumping has finished. Our Athenians mix the *stoko* with the contents of the plastic sacks, labelled '*Asbestis*', which has been lying on our road since the Poles left in July. This 'Polyfiller' concoction is used to fill in the cracks between the panels and to plaster the walls of the pool and the Roman steps. I am mildly alarmed that we are using Asbestos, which I had always thought was for fire protection – something which our plastic pool would not need when full of water. I later find out that *Asbestis* is the Greek word for the lime used in whitewash for painting houses.

Back at the house we find Nikos Builder on the roof working on priority two. He had already put up the beams of the frame, on which the ceiling, insulation, asphalt and tiles will lie.

Jannie and I continue with our frantic cleaning. We empty the spare room of the equipment and chemicals for the pool, sweep it and then wash it. I fit together the bed and we put on one of the two new mattresses. It fits. With the plastering in the pool going on at a leisurely pace, the idea of trying out the mattress, for a short siesta, is too tempting – until I realise that Nikos has started to nail the ceiling timbers on to the roof beams. After each plank is laid, the rat-a-tat-tat of a machine gun follows. He takes a handful of nails, stabs above the beam, bangs with his hammer and moves on until the plank is secure. Nikos's hammer is running red hot. By half past three, the ceiling wood is in place. He leaves for a well-earned rest.

Meanwhile George has a cigarette and watches Pavlos plaster some more. Our new pool builders work at a different tempo from the original Polish team, but by evening, they have completely sealed the sides.

With two days to go, we are still confident. We have some security, some more roof and the start of a completed pool. It is time to order the food for the party – but for how many? I count up: John, Peter and the three Nikos plus partners gives me ten. I phone Pavlos. This time his daughter, Maria, answers. Thank goodness, as she speaks some English.

"How many are coming to the party?" I ask.

"What party?" she replies.

"Didn't your father tell you that we will be celebrating on Sunday night?"

"No."

"Please can *you* organise your family?" I plead. She agrees.

We therefore must assume the number of wall builders will be between zero and five. It is time to take the plunge. We drive up to Georgy Porgy's in the village. He is delighted to see us. His pleasure turns to ecstasy when we order chicken, lamb, pork, home-made burgers and spicy 'village' sausage – fifteen portions of each.

"How many people are coming to the party?" he asks.

"Fifteen," I reply.

"I think you go 'Boomp'," he replies, demonstrating a growing stomach, which explodes.

"But Greeks like their meat," I suggest. We cut the seventy-five portions to thirty-five.

We sit outside in the street under the moon which gives the village an eerie feeling. The chicken from the spit melts in the mouth. Georgy Porgy goes off on his scooter to get a flagon of his own special wine.

Jannie and I then review progress. "There is still far too much dust around," she says. "I want a vacuum cleaner."

"Agreed."

"Des has nowhere proper to sit," she adds. "Being pregnant is hard enough, but it helps if one has a comfortable chair."

"Agreed."

Work is over for the day and we sit and just relax. Opposite us the clothes shop is closing for the night and down the street the cafenion is doing good business. We say hello to a Dutch couple, who have bought an old house in the village and have started to renovate it. They are surely the first of many foreigners who will come in their retirement. We amble back to our car, which we park at the entrance to the village. A few '*kalisperas*', good evenings, are replied to in kind. We have come a long way since Easter when we knew no-one.

Friday 7 September, 2 full days to go

I wake up, bright eyed, at four to plan the day. In which order should we work? We must pay IKA, the National Insurance Organisation; pay the concrete supplier, Proskyr; pick up our temporary gates; get food and dishes for the party; buy a Hoover and a chair for Des. I then think what Nikos should do: finish the roof; build our northern defensive wall; put up the gates; and supply electricity to the pool. I then remember the pool must be filled with water – I must ask head pool man George how long this takes. Assuming the liner is fitted today, we have twenty-four hours to fill it from the mains before Peter arrives. I fall asleep again, and get up while it is still dark to clear a way from the road through the rubbish and rubble left from the building works and the packaging discarded by the pool builders.

As we leave for town our two Albanians are hard at work and the bosses are away. Assistant pool man Pavlos is rubbing down the walls of the pool and Nikos Builder's assistant Kostas is carrying up the tiles for the roof and the bricks and concrete blocks for the northern defences. Nikos has disappeared but promises to be back later. I tell Kostas to remind him I want '*treis tripes sto tiho*', three holes in the wall, to let the water off the pergola terrace. I think he understands. Pool boss George has gone to town to meet the morning flight from Athens, which should be carrying our test equipment.

We find Nikos Mechanikos deep in paperwork. He's not happy. "My secretary normally fills out the IKA ledgers."

The sheets have been designed as data entry documents. A header entry describes the employer and the work to be carried out. Each line contains the worker's name and number, a code and number of days for the work carried out, and the rate for the task, which varies according to whether it is manual or non-manual. The total contribution is broken down into a number of amounts, one for each benefit the worker can claim. All the amounts have to be cross cast and totalled down to agree with the sum of the totals for each benefit column. Nikos then repeats the same entries on each worker's IKA receipt book with a copy to accompany the ledger with a total payment. Having completed the books for Pavlos's team, he moves on to the steel workers. No wonder he needs a secretary. He hands over everything for us to take to the IKA office.

We then turn to the subject of the concrete poured in our absence. I have calculated it at 17 cubic metres. We have enough money.

"John, I am afraid the base of the extension needed another 41 cubic metres. It saved us from building foundations, as a single story building doesn't need foundations for earthquake protection if you make the base strong enough."

I have no alternative but to accept their figures. It confirms that the owner should always be present when concrete is poured. Even more seriously, I had assumed that Nikos Builder would pay, but that isn't the case.

Having robbed the bank, we go to IKA. The cashier on the ground floor sends us upstairs. My blonde friend is busy so I join another queue. I'm told to go downstairs again, where I am directed back up to the first floor. I wait for my friend. My problems seem minor to the English girl who was managing a bar owned by a Greek. She had only found out at the end of her first month that she has to pay IKA from her management fee.

The receipts for the workers are checked against my ledger, which is stamped as being in order. My next job is to pay but I'm told to come back within fifteen working days of Monday 10th. I now understand the chaos of the first day we came to the office. Twice a month work stops throughout Greece. One is for getting IKA ledgers stamped; the other is for paying the dues. What a crazy system! However, I insist on immediate payment and am sent down to the cashier again.

In case he orders me upstairs again, I check with my blonde friend whether I should come back – she thinks I'm flirting.

Our next stop is to pick up the temporary security gates. These turn out to be one metre square aluminium frames holding aluminium mesh. I ask about pillars on which the gates would hang. I am told they could be ready by Monday. I decide that some security is better than no security, so we load our gates into the car and make for Profi to buy the vacuum cleaner.

On our way, we pass a furniture shop, called "Orient". On impulse we go in to buy a chair for our pregnant daughter-in-law and come out with a three-piece bamboo suite – comfortable, attractive and at a sale price. If one is to spend thousands on a swimming pool, why not spend a couple of hundred on some furniture? It is the first we have bought in the thirty years we have lived in Corfu. Initially, everything was built in. Then we rented out the house for a few years and the agent provided four ugly metal chairs which had slowly rusted away. Spiros, our neighbour, then added a decaying leather sofa, which we returned this year when we had the great bust-up. Only our own marble coffee table with the inlaid chess board remained. It has been knocked over and glued together on numerous occasions. Our shack is on the road to palatial status.

Back at home, Nikos has put up the north wall, but with no holes for the water to run off the terrace. Speaking poor Greek to an Albanian is obviously no good. This minor problem doesn't worry Nikos who produces his miniature pneumatic drill and blasts a hole in the wall.

George and Pavlos are fitting the pool liner in a fairly laid-back manner. George has taken the supervisory role and lets the Albanian do most of the work. I phone Alexos to question progress.

"Will your men be finished today, as I want to start filling the pool tonight?" I ask.

"I'm sorry, but George wants an extra half day. He hadn't been told about the Roman steps."

What appears to be a few hours work by both men to complete the installation of the liner that evening is just speculation on my part. We now have just one worker and a manager. I tell George I want to start filling the pool overnight, as it must be full by midnight tomorrow.

"Where is the water coming from?" he asks.

"From the mains, via our gravity tank and the garden hose," I reply.

"That will take forty-eight hours."

"Can we use your pump to empty our *sterna*?"

"OK, but it will still take twenty-four hours," George replies.

It is becoming obvious that Peter and Des will arrive to find a completed pool which is empty. Even more serious, our Athenians will have left before their equipment has been tested. But worst of all will be Nikos Mechanikos, who will be gloating over the failure of the plastic pool.

That evening we decide to eat at Theodoros on the beach, even if we are told that we will never finish the pool on time. On the way, as fate would have it, we pass Alexandra, who owns a lean-to, selling trinkets to the tourists. As many of the shopkeepers do, she is sitting outside chatting with her neighbours.

"Hello, John, how is the great pool?" she asks with genuine interest. "I see it every day when I come down from the village."

"We have a small problem. We need to fill it before our son comes tomorrow night."

"Don't worry! My uncle supplies water to everyone in the area. How many tanker loads do you want?" she asks.

"Fifteen cubic metres," I reply.

She goes inside to make a phone call and returns with bad news.

"Uncle Pavlos is in Italy seeing his son, but I can get you someone else to deliver the water."

"Who?" I ask impressed with the local organisation.

"Nikos Grammenos, the bulldozer driver."

We are delighted. We use her phone to call Nikos Bulldozer, our hero of the building project.

"Can you deliver a tanker load of water at one tomorrow?"

"Of course, John, no problem," he replies.

Jannie and I now know that we will win the race. We almost skip down the road and along the beach. Even though it is dark since the moon has not appeared over Garouna, it's time for a swim, a half-litre of Fotis's excellent wine and some pan-fried fish from Maria.

Fotis is in a philosophical mood.

"John, why do you want a pool, when you have the sea to swim in?" he asks.

"Because nowadays there are so many people on the beach."

"That's why I like it here in the winter. Every day, I come down from the village and sit and watch the waves rolling in."

"And you think that is the most important thing in life?" I ask.

"Yes, of course. But the others in Agios Gordis don't agree. They all want to make more and more money."

"Sometimes they have to make the money to pay off the bank," I suggest.

"But does it make them happier?" he asks rhetorically. "Look at Spiros Grammenos at the Pink Palace, he is still working in his seventies – to pay off the money he has borrowed. Don't tell me that all his development has enhanced Agios Gordis."

I cannot argue with him as I can see both sides' case. Perhaps he would like to return to the days of his childhood before all the building on the beach. At that moment his younger brother Tassos arrives. Alexos Hirdaris, the pool engineer, has told me that Tassos coaches his son at tennis.

"How is the tennis coach?" I ask.

"How do you know about that?" he replies.

I tell him. "You must play my son Peter. He arrives tomorrow."

Fotis returns with a second half-litre of wine. The conversation becomes more animated. "Is he any good?" Tassos asks.

"He's better than you," I reply provocatively. In fact, Alexos has told me how good the tennis coach is.

"In which case, what will you bet on the match?"

"Anything you like; I know he can beat you."

"OK, then. I like your car – I'll play for that," answers Tassos.

"But I don't like *your* car," I reply, referring to his battered Suzuki jeep. "What will you put up?"

I am very confident. So is he. "If Peter wins, you can have the restaurant."

We shake on our wager and Jannie pulls me home.

Saturday 8 September, 1 full day to go

My enthusiasm of last night has waned. This morning, George will install the 'filterbox' – the pump and filtration plant. But he won't be able to test it until we have filled the pool. As we cannot put water in until the liner has been fixed, I decide we need a crisis. I fit the hose to the tap behind the house and lead it to the pool. We'll start filling before they have finished. As the water rises out of the deep end, they will be faced with imminent drowning.

On the stroke of nine o'clock, I turn on the tap and a delicious clear stream pours out. The feeling of relief overwhelms me. The battle has been won. Laughing, I turn to the pool team, George and Pavlos.

"Let's celebrate. Two cups of coffee?"

"Why not?" replies George.

By the time their coffee has cooled – Greeks like food and drink tepid – it is half past nine. I take the blue and red mugs out to reward progress. Pavlos has fitted the liner to the side of the bottom Roman step and George has installed the filterbox case. I check on the water flowing from the hose – it isn't. The gravity tank is empty and the mains supply has stopped. Now I certainly have a crisis even if it's not the one I planned. It is pointless to wait for the water to restart as the problem is either Alamanos & Son fixing a burst pipe or a cut in the supply which we frequently get in the autumn.

George is not concerned. We lower a jug into the *sterna* and it fills with crystal clear water, a collection of the rain during the previous winter. He inserts a pipe into the great concrete box and then switches his pump on. Out rushes a cascade of filthy water – he hasn't cleared the pipes of the leaves which had collected when he emptied the pool when he first arrived. We have progressed from a pristine puddle to a murky pond.

Moments later, Fred turns up.

"Hiya, buddy, I've brought my chainsaw. Which trees am I going to cut down today?"

I look around the property. Lots of olives remain but the poplars have gone.

"Fred, we've run out of trees. Today is clean-up day. There's rubble all round the house. Can you sort out the back yard and the olive tree terrace?"

I sense he's disappointed. Clearing jungles and cutting down forests is what he prefers. Now he is a menial garbage collector.

As we are leaving for town – shops close at four on Saturdays – Nikos Builder arrives.

"I'll connect up the electricity for the pump today," he promises. I can see that there is no way that he will be responsible for an empty pool at the party tomorrow.

"And then we'll put up some railings to stop my grandson from falling off the pool terrace?" I respond.

"OK, John, and then I'll have a swim," he says, adding with his wicked grin. "I've brought you some wine – it's my father's, it's excellent."

He turns the screw cap on the five litre demijohn and pours me a glass. He's right. A quick sip tells me that we won't want much more wine at the party. Sinarades red is the best on the island.

"What are we going to eat?" he asks.

I tell him about the meat from Georgy Porgy.

"I'll make a large village salad as well," I suggest.

"And what about the octopus – it's my favourite. And get some beer; we'll drink that as well."

With our shopping list now agreed, we set off for town. Dimitra sells the best feta, our friendly greengrocer has fresh vegetables and fruit and Diellas has the cheapest drink. We stock up with their special-offer beer, packs of 'six for the price of five' water and bottles of *Makedonikos* wine for the cognoscenti.

We make for home. On the long straight with Agii Deka ahead, Tassos roars past in his jeep. He waves his tennis racquet at us – he's obviously been coaching in town. As we climb up the hairpin bends, I glance across out of the passenger window and see Georgy Porgy creeping up beside us on his scooter. He indicates that Jannie should open the window.

"I have all the meat," he shouts. "Shall I bring the bread as well?"

"No, I will," I scream. "Look out!"

He swerves back behind us as a bus comes round the corner. He lives to cook the feast. We stop off at the Kastellani bakery and one of the sisters produces a small brown loaf – our standard order.

"Three large whites and three large brown," I say.

She gets the six enormous loaves – they are still warm. I pay only £1.50 – bread is good value in Greece; it has to be, as so much is eaten.

"Your son comes today?" she asks. I had obviously told everyone on the island. "He has big family?"

"No, we are having a party tomorrow." She likes that answer as well.

At exactly one o'clock the hero in the water tanker arrives. Parking above the house, Nikos Bulldozer takes a short cut through Bellevedere Apartments. Spiros stops him and complains that building work has been starting when his guests were asleep. Noone wakes up before nine o'clock in the shadow of the mountain. A thick pipe is dropped down from on high and put in the pool. Gravity does the rest. As the two Nikoses drink their coffees, talk turns to tomorrow.

"Are you bringing your wife to the party?" I ask the older ever-laughing Nikos Builder.

"No, we are having a few problems. But I'll bring a young friend."

I have heard good comments about his 'beautiful' wife, and I am intrigued and rather alarmed about a 'young friend' coming. Still it is not the moment to discuss matrimonial problems. I guess the cause – he's an all-Greek man. Whether he is laying bricks, hammering nails or driving his battered truck, mini moped or highly polished Mitsubishi saloon – he is a bundle of energy.

Turning to Nikos Bulldozer, our reliable and solid villager, I ask about his party partner.

"I'm coming with a friend as well." He laughs and points to Nikos Builder. "An old friend! I might bring another friend; his wife is English and he speaks your language, John."

I'm sad that we might end up with three men rather than two men and their wives. However, either combination would eat the same. The water has risen to the first Roman step. I reckon our Albanian liner man, who is working on the last step, will not drown after all. Though I had ordered only one tanker load, Nikos Bulldozer is happy to return with another.

214

Fred, meanwhile, is forlorn. He is not his bubbling self. He has done a good clearing job but is obviously unhappy. "The problem with Greek builders is that they never clean up their rubbish."

"I agree, Fred, but now is not the time to ask them to do it. The building work is still not finished."

"But that's typical – they never finish."

"Fred, I think the two Nikoses have been fantastic. Anyway, something else is bugging you. What is it, my old mate?" I ask.

"That Bulldozer bloke ignores me. I don't think he likes me."

Working in a foreign country and not speaking the language cannot be easy. I reckon all immigrant workers – and Fred is one – should have thick skins. But Fred doesn't; he's really a softie.

"Don't worry, Fred. I like you!" I reply.

I give him his money and we down a last beer. He won't come again for a couple of weeks, when we will get down to clearing the rest of the battleground.

Everyone is hard at work. Pavlos is finishing the last step. George has fixed the 'Filterblock' and Nikos has laid the cable under the void of the pool surrounds from the annexe to the deep end. George connects one end to his pump and the other to the consumer unit.

We now move on to safety systems. The wall between the veranda and pool has been built, so Nikos fixes the two gates – one at the top of the stairs from the road and the other onto the pool terrace. I park a couple of redundant metal chairs at each end of the veranda, one at the gap to the olive tree terrace and the other in the empty door of the annexe. We can now trap Sean on the veranda.

Meanwhile Nikos Bulldozer has returned with the second tanker load. Water pours out again. We watch it slowly rise and at the critical moment it flows over the skimmer in the filtration unit. George turns on the motor. It works. The two Nikoses and I cheer.

"Now you have a swim, John," orders Nikos Builder.

The water feels freezing, but who cares? I creep in down the Roman Steps, inch by inch, and then swim an immaculate length. I stand on the ledge above the deep end and look down to the beach far below, then turn to the mountains to the south. The sun is still fierce in the sky and is mirrored in the sparkling sea. This is total bliss. To me, the job has been completed, but George reckons we need a top-up.

"*Alli dheo ponti*," he says. Two more points, which I think is slang for two more centimetres. The *sterna* is empty, the mains supply has been cut – there is no alternative to Nikos Bulldozer getting another tanker load.

The other Nikos is finished for the day – he needs his siesta.

It is now school time for the new pool owners. George produces a manual, which luckily is in English. He points to the pictures and questions us on our comprehension.

"OK?" he asks.

"*Ola kala!*" I reply – all is good. As the pages are turned our dialogue continues. One can now understand how the Americans turned the Greek immigrants' standard statement '*ola kala*" to OK. In truth, I find the lecture boring; I much prefer to try out my new toy.

Jannie, who, thank goodness, is the family instruction book reader, is eventually satisfied. We've been shown the chemicals, the test equipment, the Filterbox and the Hoover and net for cleaning the pool. She passes the test for the two of us – I cannot read instructions.

We stand on the veranda, under its gorgeous wooden rafters and look out over the safety wall and the crystal clear pool to the shining sea beyond. Only Nikos Builder's standard ditty is adequate.

"*Ola kala kai ola oraia*" – all is good and all is beautiful.

Nikos Bulldozer arrives and we fill the pool to the brim and pour the rest in the *sterna*. It gives us an emergency supply if we have further water cuts.

With Nikos Builder asleep, the pool men gone and Jannie making beds for our family who arrive at two in the morning, I have one last project – the completion of the safety measures. We can trap Sean on the veranda but once he gets on the pool terrace, he could be over the four metre drop into the olive trees before one could say "Stop".

Fred's jungle-clearing and my bamboo-trimming now bear fruit. With the wire left by the steel men, I bind the bamboo into a 3x1 metre mesh, which I erect on the edge of the pool terrace in a Greek version of a wattle fence. The last two rusting chairs block the fall into the cavern where the ramp will be built and on the path between pool and veranda. I now have my second line of defence.

With the sun now setting, I look at my work and see, through the olive trees, a movement on our road below. Nikos is returning to check that all is complete. He looks at my crude construction.

"John, that fence is very good."

"You mean, I could be a builder?" I ask.

"Why not?"

"Because I'll charge more than one of your Albanians!"

"But you make very good coffee as well," he adds.

We stand laughing, admiring his curvaceous roof over the huge veranda, my plastic pool and the new views from the pool terrace to the sunset in the west and the mountain to the south.

"Are you going for a swim, Nikos?" I ask.

He puts his hand in the water.

"No, it's too cold. Maybe tomorrow."

Unusually for Nikos, I think this *'avrio'* is the Greek version. He leaves in a happy mood – his work complete. He can now enjoy his weekend of pleasure, which will culminate in our party tomorrow.

I start trying to seat our guests in the traditionally western fashion – alternating women and men with English speakers intermingled. I am totally ignored. The four builders sit at one end and leave the rest to sort themselves out.

The moment has arrived. Accustomed as I am to public speaking, I rise. This is only the second speech I have made in a foreign language

Celebrating the victory

Night flights are the bane of Corfu tourism. To cut fares, most operators using Gatwick leave London before midnight and return early next morning. The eight hour round trip (including the hour on the ground in Corfu) enables the aircraft to be used on another route during the day. The downside is carried by the passengers. Arriving at two in the morning is bad enough, but spending one's last night in Corfu airport must spoil the holiday. For us, a few hours sleep before picking up our friends and a good meal at Greek hours before we leave them at the airport in the early hours causes little inconvenience.

After a tin of sardines and a thick slice from our fresh bread, we go to bed at nine. Moments later the phone goes. It can't be one of our Greek friends – they are already on their way out to dinner. Perhaps it's Peter – Des's baby is due soon. I pick up the receiver.

"I'm coming now. OK?" says the voice in Greek. I'm not expecting anyone.

"Who is that?" I ask.

"Georgy Porgy – I have your food."

"But today is Saturday," I reply.

"Yes?" he answers.

"Our party is on Sunday," I explain.

There is a long silence. I can see a huge pile of aluminium boxes on the counter and the open-mouthed cook behind. "I'm sorry. Yes, you are right. Your party is tomorrow."

"Are you still OK for tomorrow?" I ask.

"Yes, OK. No problem."

"But what about the food you've cooked?"

219

There is another long pause. I think a conference is going on in the village. "My family will eat everything."

Sunday 6 September, zero hour

We return to bed, to sleep and to wake. Before we leave for town, we put on the lights in the pool. An eerie blue glow rises up.

We drive to the airport and, on time, the plane arrives. I go out to watch the passengers come through passport control. Now that Greece is in the EU, there is no problem; everyone is waved through, until it is Des's turn. A Jamaican passport is a novelty. Greek bureaucracy springs into action. The immigration officer picks up his phone – he must be calling his superiors. Eventually the boss arrives and checks her visa.

"No problem. Welcome to Greece," he says.

I give each of them a big hug. "Sorry about that, Peter. It's just the Greek officials doing their thing."

"Don't worry, Daddy. If the supervisor hadn't been called, I would have insisted he was. The trouble we all had in getting the visa is surely worth a bit of appreciation."

We laugh, but I remember how Des can come to England but then cannot go on to France or Greece. If Britain had signed the Schengen agreement, there would have been no problem at all. But we still are not really in Europe, I think. I also remember her first time in England – immigration at Gatwick refused to let her stay. At a visit to the House of Commons, with Peter and Des, to plead her case I was asked by my MP: "Are you sure you want your son to have her as a girl friend?"

Des is happy to get out of the plane – her bump is even bigger than with Sean – and he was the largest baby Kingston Hospital had delivered. Tourist class seats are made for slim singles. On her previous visit she liked Corfu. It reminded her of home – the mountains coming down to the sea, and the donkeys! Sean is subdued. He holds on to his Daddy for dear life. He doesn't like the crowds pushing around the luggage carousel.

With the car loaded with the passengers, pushchair and suitcases full of baby food and pampers, we crawl over the mountain and stop on the road below. The moon is now six days from full but strong enough to pour a glow over the unmade road which rises where the jungle used to be.

"Fantastic," says Peter.

We pick our way up over the boulders and dried up valleys, which will soon be covered by concrete. Beyond the huge mound of rubble, the veranda looms high.

"Fantastic," says our son.

We climb the steps and stop at the top. He looks at the glowing pool.

"Fantastic," he says.

The three piece suite is at the end of the long veranda. Peter and Des collapse onto the sofa.

"Fantastic," he says again.

"It is really comfortable," adds Des.

"I'll open the gate," I suggest. "It's part of the safety measures for Sean."

"Fantastic," he says yet again.

We go out and test the water.

"Ouch! That's cold," he says. "But it is still fantastic."

We put on our trunks and dive into the pool.

"OK, Peter, I know what you are going to say," says Jannie as she watches her two men swim a couple of lengths, but it is time for bed.

Early next morning, we are woken by swearing coming from our minute bathroom. "Oh, shit," shouts Peter.

I creep out to investigate. In the dark he has tripped over the chemical toilet. He points to the sanitary solution to our summer with no soakaway.

"Daddy, you must sort this out. Des won't be happy."

Our guests slept late. At ten o'clock, I hear more noise from the bathroom. Des has taken one look at the bucket. It almost makes her throw up. In a huff, she disappears out of the house to return a long time later.

"The Ladies loo is behind the last olive tree on the left," she announces.

She had found our neighbour's olive grove and was now a happy guest again. I didn't mention the snakes, whose home she has probably disturbed. Her reaction to lizards on her last visit was bad enough. Jamaicans seem to think they are devils. It doesn't help that I like most creepy crawlies. At least our spiders can't kill – although she doesn't believe me. She reckons most are poisonous.

"And how does your toilet compare with home?" I ask.

I remember my visits into the bushes, when we celebrated a fantastic New Year in the Central Highlands of Jamaica with her family.

"Your view is better!" she admits.

Peter joins me on the pool terrace, which is bathed with sun. "I remember when I was little, before we planted the trees in front of the house, we had this fantastic view, just of Ortholithi and the sea. From out here, you can now see right round to the mountains to the south. When you've fixed up this terrace and added a pergola, you and Mummy can have breakfast here as the sun comes over the mountain."

After breakfast, we prepare for the pool. Peter pumps up the pink lilo for Des. She has already announced the water is too cold. Sean is then fitted with his life jacket. He is like his mother and lets us know what he thinks about his new bath; he shrieks in fear. He refuses to get out of Peter's arms. But he likes it when his Mummy, on her big plastic float, joins him. Before long he is sitting on the top Roman step – it's as deep as his bath at home.

"This is fun," I reckon he is thinking. "Daddy and Pops are playing with a ball in the pool. I would like to do that."

The ball is moved to the veranda and Arsenal plays Liverpool. Peter passes to Sean. "Kick it at Pops, Michael Owen," Peter calls.

"Whoops! It's gone through the gate," thinks Sean.

David Seaman runs after it before it goes in the pool.

Sean shrieks with delight at the fun.

"Have another kick," says Peter. "No, not that way!"

The ball disappears down the steps over the boxes wall. The three boys chase it but it is bouncing down our rutted road, across the main road and over its high retaining wall into Michael's Romantic View below. We go in search and find it in his pool. Michael, the ultimate football fanatic, who trains the local junior team, is impressed.

"Sean has talent," he says. "Can I sign him up?"

He is more interested in getting his ball back. The Scandinavian girls, on their sunbeds, are impressed as well. Sean, with his curly hair and beautiful brown skin, is gorgeous.

Thirty years ago, when Peter was Sean's age, we would have lunch at Theodoros on the beach, while Louise and Peter played. Peter now wants to pass on his experience to his son. Jannie and I sip wine. Des drinks lemonade and waits for our Greek salad while watching her two men play ball on the beach.

"Darling, this takes us back, doesn't it?" Jannie says.

"The sand is the same, the sea is the same – alright, there are people on our beach now. But who cares?"

"I love it here, Mummy," says Des.

We watch father and son playing in the sand. Even the castles they make are like the ones we used to make all those years ago. They stand in the shallows and the little waves brush their feet. The sandbank protects them in their little swimming pool. We are all so happy.

Tassos brings the food and we call to Peter to join us. But Sean won't come. He's found a friend – a three year old blonde who, spellbound, is watching this little curly-topped bundle of fun. He kicks the sand; she laughs. He kicks it again; she laughs again. She jumps up and down; he jumps up and down. She dances a jig; he falls over. She laughs; he laughs as well. She puts her head in the sand to do a somersault. He bends over and does the same. She has her bottom sticking up in the air; his sticks skyward as well.

"Do you think he knows what to do next?" asks Des.

She laughs; Peter laughs; Jannie laughs and I laugh. I call over to him.

"Sean, don't worry; be happy!"

"I don't think you need worry, Daddy; he's very happy."

I call Tassos over. "Here is your opponent in the big tennis match." I turn to Peter. "You had better beat him or else we lose our car."

"Daddy, I'll beat him because I want his restaurant."

We return to the house for a siesta. I am dreaming of Jamaica – beating drums. But the music is not reggae. It's the rat-a-tat-tat of a machine gun. I wake up and realise that the noise is coming from outside. It is raining. The veranda roof acts like a drum skin. Once the shower ends, we venture out to see the damage. The road up to the house is covered in mud – sticky grey clay mud. Where it is worst, we lay parts of the old roof down as duck boards. I silently thank the Greek builders for leaving their rubbish behind. The party can still go ahead. Our guests will be able to get up to the house.

As the sun disappears behind mounting cumulonimbus clouds, we enter the final lap of the great race. Peter, with Des's help and Sean's hindrance, takes control of the tables. We move out the original wooden one with its two benches and put plastic tables at each end. With three on each bench and five plastic seats for each plastic table, they lay places for sixteen guests. Everything is plastic – water and wine glasses from Woolworths in England and matching blue plates from Corfu. He then moves on to music; Des's contribution to the new house is a ghetto blaster. Each of us chooses our favourite music: Jannie goes for the Beatles; Des wants Bob Marley and Toots and the Myrtals; Peter likes Motown; and I prefer Theodorakis. Sean likes them all. Dancing to each, he is already showing that he has his mother's rhythm.

Jannie, meanwhile, is putting plates of cut meats, Corfu salami and *nouboulo*, the delicious smoked pork loin, on the table. These are followed by bowls of *taramasalata*, the cod's roe paste, *melitsanosalata*, the mashed aubergine puree, *tirokafteri*, the peppery cheese mash, and *tzatziki*, made of yoghurt, cucumber and mint. We in the West would call these starters, but the Greeks ignore order in a meal and eat anything at hand.

My job is the *horiatiki*, the village salad, which must be crude in construction and fresh in flavour. I cut up firm but sweet tomatoes in great chunks. The tasty green peppers are halved, deseeded and then sliced in semicircles. Cucumbers, picked today, are skinned and chopped into finger thick sections. Mild red onions are peeled and then sliced across into rings, which fall apart when pressed. With the practical pleasure over, I throw everything onto three great oval plates in a melee of reds and greens with an artist's gay abandon. Liberally sprinkled oregano wafts a pungent scent over the salad.

I then move on to the part which tickles my taste buds. Slabs are carved from the huge block of feta, still oozing water from its life in a five kilogram tin. These are broken into mouth-size pieces and scattered over the vegetables. I chose *Dodoni* or *Ipiros*, the slightly sweeter cheese. I would have preferred *Choponakis*, which is creamy not flaky and mild not sharp, but it is difficult to find. To match the white, I finish up with the black – fleshy, spicy *kalamata* olives, each with its little tail. The trick with this most delicious of fruit is to fill a jar with the black berries and pour on olive oil. A sprig of rosemary can be added for taste. After a week they have swollen to succulent additions to the *meze* plate, or become a meal in themselves with coarse brown bread.

We decant Nikos Builder's demijohn into three plastic bottles – one for each table. With a couple of dozen cans of beers and some bottles of *Makedonikos* wine as well, I am sure we will satisfy our hard-drinking workers.

The sun has set, though we haven't seen it go down. It is time to put the finishing touches to my speech which, to my embarrassment and the others' amusement, will be delivered in Greek. I collect up the presents; in Greece, I have been told, the host gives the guests a little something. I at last sit down to relax, sipping some of Nikos's nectar. His father has done us proud.

Peter has lit paraffin lamps along our road up to the villa to guide our visitors on our wooden ramps. We are ready. It starts to rain – hard. We are in for a storm.

At nine o'clock, our two local Nikoses arrive – without partners. A few minutes later Nikos Mechanikos drives up with Anna and we wait.

"Is Pavlos coming?" asks my engineer.

"I hope so," I reply.

He grunts. I'm not sure what he means. We are now eight; half the number we might expect. "And who else is coming?"

"Only Pavlos's party."

He doesn't say what I am thinking, but I am sure it is on his mind. Pavlos could be up to his old tricks. The three Nikoses don't mind – it'll mean more meat for each of them. They drink their beers and we wait. The rain gets stronger; the storm has arrived.

"John, *eho ena problima*," I hear a voice from below cry. If it's a problem it has to be Pavlos. I go to investigate. George Segal, as always, elegant in white shirt and trousers, is leading two fine looking dark haired ladies up to the house, over the steeplechase course. The wives of our wall builders are an asset at any dinner party. Pavlos follows with an elderly couple, who turn out to be George's parents.

"*Ti eenay to problima sas?*" I ask.

"*O adelphos tou Georgiou!*" George's brother is the problem.

Pavlos and George go down to the car below and I hear a great argument going on. It turns out that the brother is disabled and very shy. He doesn't want to come to the party. He is coaxed and helped up the road to be welcomed by a happy throng.

The phone rings. "Are you ready?" asks Georgy Porgy.

"Of course," I reply.

Five minutes later, we hear a scooter coming down the mountain and then Spiros, our chef's son, arrives carrying foil boxes so high that he can barely see where he is going. We put them on the table.

I start trying to seat our guests in the traditionally western fashion – alternating women and men with English speakers intermingled. I am totally ignored. The four builders sit at one end and leave the rest to sort themselves out. With George on my left and Nikos Mechanikos on my right, Peter and George's father share out the ladies. The feast begins. I decide the Greeks are the ultimate carnivores, as chops, steaks and chunks of chicken plus home-made burgers and spicy sausages are devoured. An occasional fork is jabbed into the salad and huge chunks of bread are broken off. Wine and beer is consumed in copious quantities. We are all very happy.

The moment has arrived. Accustomed as I am to public speaking, I rise. This is only the second speech I have made in a foreign language – the first, in Danish, a language which I have now forgotten, was at our wedding.

"Welcome, friends and wives!" I start.

"And mother, father and brother," Pavlos chips in. I didn't say that as I hadn't written them down in my speech. They hadn't been expected. They were still welcome.

"Thank you for finishing everything in time for Peter and Des."

Eyes turn to the end of the tables and "*oraia*" is called as the men comment on Des's undoubted beauty. Neither Peter nor Des understands what they are saying but both smile.

"As a reward for your wonderful work, I have brought you …" I continue.

"Dollars," calls Pavlos – and the men roar with laughter.

"No! Presents."

"Bravo, John," they respond.

For each I have a framed photograph as a memento of their achievements: the wall builders sitting down under the olive trees drinking coffee, with litter spread around; Nikos Mechanikos enjoying Jannie's Danish chicken and asparagus; Nikos Bulldozer celebrating with Lefteris and Marinos after scaling the boxes wall; and Nikos, our wonder builder, stripped to the waist being helped by Kostas the Albanian.

"Pavlos and George, to each of you I also give new lorries, which will not break down." I handed them model trucks.

"To Nikos, the hero, I give you a bulldozer." I'm glad I hadn't shown it to Sean. As quarter Irish, half Jamaican and a fan of Danny the Digger, he would have wanted to keep it.

"To Nikos, the best builder in Corfu, I have a new moped." I had found a gold painted metal model of a Victorian bicycle – I am sure he didn't mind my poetic licence.

"To Nikos, my engineer, I have two presents."

"Bravo, Nikos," the workers cry. I think they like his down to earth approach to construction.

"Today, he drives a BMW. Tomorrow, he has a Mercedes." I pass him a toy, depicting some monster saloon.

"Nikos, thank you for putting up with me: my plastic pool, my telephone calls, my request for a schedule. But most of all, thank you for not doing what you said you would do so often."

"Shoot you!" says Nikos Mechanikos.

"Why not?" calls Pavlos.

"I have here a gun," I continue. "I am giving it to Anna, who will keep it in case you really want to kill me. Then you can use my pistol – it is made of plastic."

Great cheers follow and I sit down.

Anna, the long suffering wife of the engineer, turns to Jannie, the long suffering wife of the client. "Jannie, tonight has been Greek theatre. The stage is perfect – the actors sitting round the table, eating and drinking under the beautiful wooden roof of your veranda, which keeps out the pouring rain. Thankfully, we have not had tragedy, but we have had drama and comedy, but most of all love – your love of our island."

Post Script

13 August 2004

The Olympics are completed on time. Bravo, Greece.

HAVE YOU READ ...

In 1966, John Waller and his Danish wife visit the island. In the days before charter flights and package tours, Corfu is 'heaven on earth'. In 1971 they buy a plot of land above undiscovered Agios Gordis on the west coast and build a modest summer house. They discover the sometimes high financial and emotional cost of possessing 'Greek Walls'.

COMING IN 2006

John Waller's first novel, a story of love and hate, is set in Ireland in the 1920s and based on a relative's eye-witness account of the arrival of the 'Black and Tans':

"If a police barracks is burned or if the barracks already occupied is not suitable, then the best house in the locality is to be commandeered, the occupants thrown into the gutter. Let them die there – the more the merrier.

Should the order ("Hands Up") not be immediately obeyed, shoot and shoot with effect. If the persons approaching (a patrol) carry their hands in their pockets, or are in any way suspicious-looking, shoot them down. You may make mistakes occasionally and innocent persons may be shot, but that cannot be helped, and you are bound to get the right parties some time. The more you shoot, the better I will like you, and I assure you no policeman will get into trouble for shooting any man." (Lt. Col. Smyth, June 1920)